Floating on air

Linda Wong

Dedication

This book is dedicated to my husband and mother without whose understanding, love and infinite patience, would never have been written.

Acknowledgements

My thanks to Professor Ian Spain and Elizabeth for allowing me to use their wedding cake on the front cover and to Jill Martin for providing Christmas Time and Happy Birthday. I would also like to thank my mother and father-in-law and Laura for their help in the preparation of this book.

Published in 1991 by Linda Wong
1 Purcell Avenue
Tonbridge
Kent TN10 4DP

©Copyright 1990 by Linda Wong
ISBN 0 9517460 0 6

All rights reserved. No part of this publication may be reproduced, stored in a retrieval system, or transmitted in any form or by any means, electronic, mechanical, photocopying, recording or otherwise without the prior written permission of the author.

Cover design by Mike Page, Tonbridge, Kent.

Photography by Wells Graphics, Tunbridge Wells, Kent.

Typesetting by Advanced Data Graphics, Sevenoaks, Kent.

Printed in Hong Kong by South China Printing Co. (1988) Ltd.

About the Author

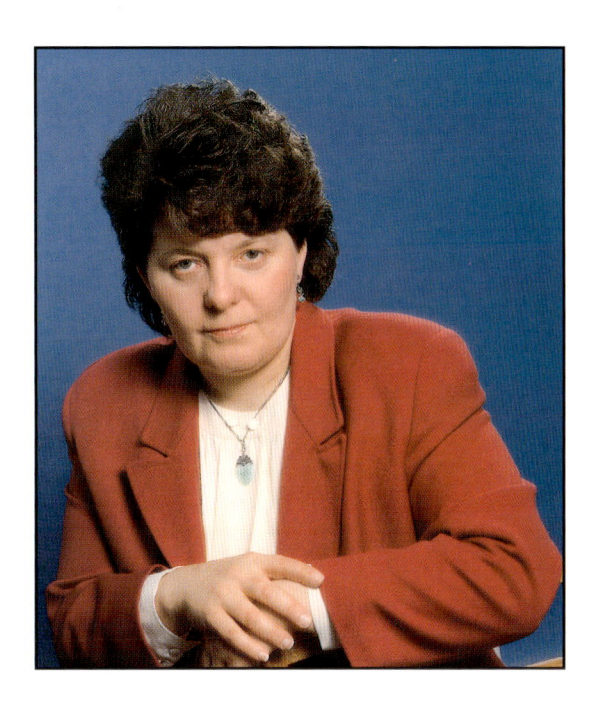

Linda has been interested in cake decoration since her early days at school. She treated this as a hobby until studying Sugarcraft at an Adult Education Centre.

This led her to join the British Sugarcraft Guild. She has won several competitions including the novice and master class sugarpaste at the B.S.G. London Exhibition.

She loved doing extension work and developed her own unique techniques for Floating Extension Work. She wished to pass on her knowledge and pleasure so decided to write this book as a guide to others.

She teaches privately and in Adult Education and also gives demonstrations to groups who are interested in Sugarcraft. She is currently studying the final year of a Certificate in Education F.E.A at Croydon College.

Contents

ABOUT THE AUTHOR 3

INTRODUCTION 5

EQUIPMENT 6

THE CAKE 8

ROYAL ICING 11

COVERING WITH MARZIPAN 13

COVERING WITH SUGARPASTE 16

PATTERN MAKING 21

RIBBON INSERTION 26

USEFUL PIPING TECHNIQUES 27

RUN-OUT TECHNIQUES 31

BRUSH EMBROIDERY 38

EXTENSION WORK 40

FLOATING EXTENSION WORK TECHNIQUES 45

EMBROIDERY AND LACE 57

VARIATIONS ON A THEME 60

CAKE DESIGNS 74

FIXED EXTENSION WORK 75
Christmas Time
Happy Birthday
Congratulations
Heart's Delight

FLOATING EXTENSION WORK 87
Merry Christmas
Lullaby
Castle in the Air
Cream Sensation
Best of Friends
Golden Showers
Kentish Scene
True Love

TABLES OF QUANTITIES 107

INDEX 108

Introduction

I have always had a love of sugarcraft and have explored the techniques involved in extension work quite extensively.

For many years I have been experimenting and perfecting my sugarcraft techniques and have developed my own technique for producing floating extension work and now feel it is time to share my secrets with others. Whether you are a novice or more experienced there is something here for you, from the Castle in the Air cake to the more complex Cream Sensation. All the cakes illustrated are accompanied by a scheme of work together with details on how they were decorated. I have also included sections covering the many techniques used in their production together with hints on how I work. These sections will prove to be of benefit if you have never used the techniques before. It is not necessary to have any experience of traditional fixed extension work before attempting the floating varieties.

So come on everyone, have a go you never know what you can achieve until you try.

Equipment

There are several items of equipment you will need in order to complete the techniques described in this book, some of which you will probably recognise, whilst others may be new to you. I have therefore included a description of most of the items shown. Always use good quality equipment as cheaper alternatives may not have the same durability and thus prove more costly in the long run.

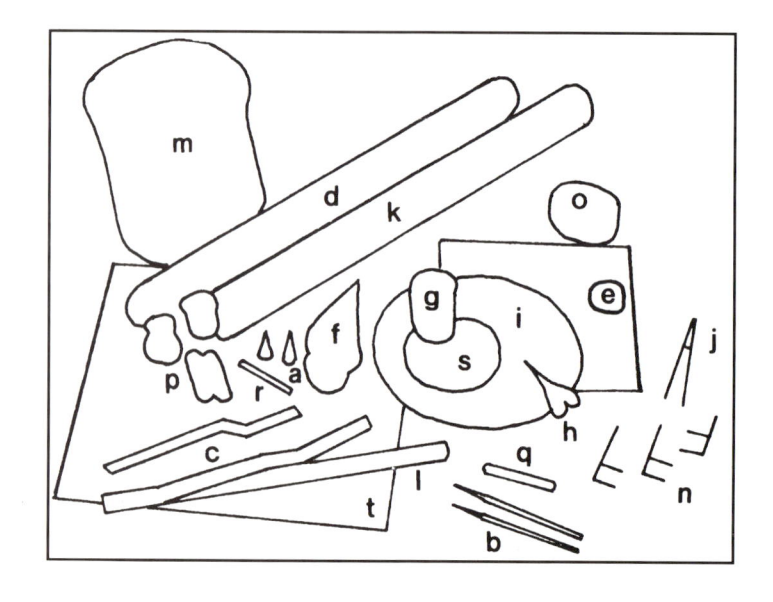

a	**Piping tubes**	The techniques shown in this book have been piped using Nos.2,1,0,00 size only.
b	**Paint brushes Size 0,1**	These are used for tidying ends and finishing extension work.
c	**Crank handled palette knives**	These come in various sizes. I find I use both palette knives, the finer for lifting lace and filigree pieces and the thicker for moving floating bridge lines.
d	**Rolling pin**	This needs to be at least 400mm (16") long.
e	**Tape measure**	
f	**Greaseproof piping bags**	
g	**Adding machine roll**	Used in the making of side patterns.
h	**Scissors**	Always ensure these are very sharp as they are used to cut paper patterns and bags.
i	**Cake drums and boards**	These come in various shapes, sizes and thicknesses.
j	**A pair of compasses**	I use this when drawing patterns for the floating bridge.
k	**Cellophane**	Always use a crease free type. I prefer not to use cling film or waxed paper for floating extension work as I find it is more difficult to remove very fine lines and lace from these.
l	**Ruler**	Also used when making patterns.
m	**Round airtight container**	This is used for storing royal icing.
n	**"L" brackets**	These are used to support the floating bridge whilst working.
o	**Plaque cutter**	Used to cut plaques from pastillage.
p	**Food colours**	Powders, paste and liquid food colours are all used at various points in this book.
q	**Spirit level**	Used to check if marzipan and sugarpaste cake coverings are level.
r	**Tube cleaner**	
s	**Ribbon**	1.5 or 3mm used as decoration around cake bases and in flower sprays.
t	**Glass sheet**	Provides a firm base for run-out work.

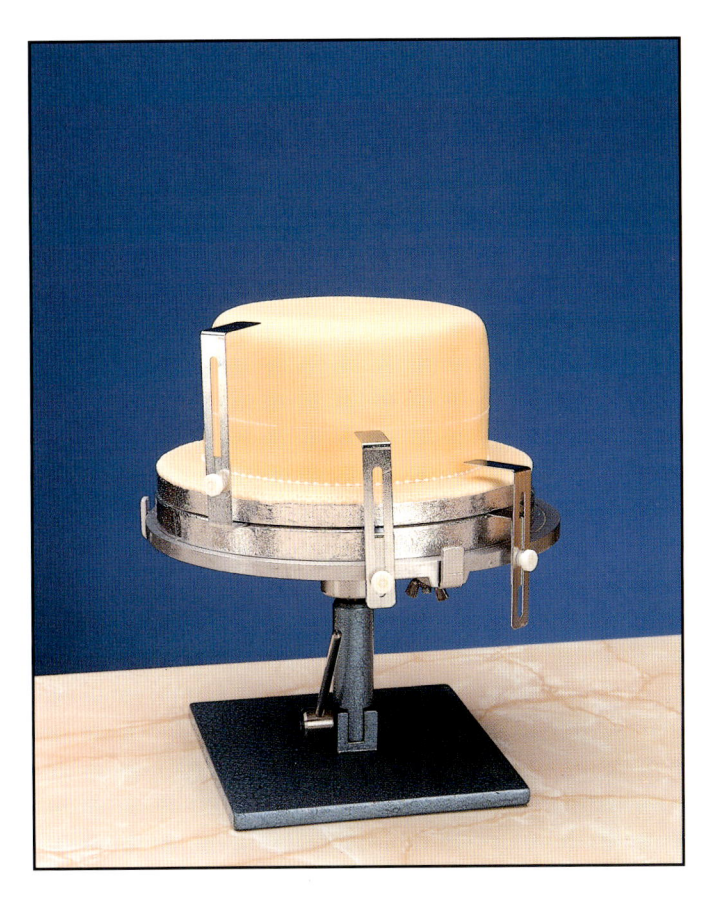

"L" Brackets

These unique brackets were designed by my husband and myself to support the floating extension work bridge. Made of stainless steel with nylon thumb nuts and screws for ease of adjustment, they are versatile and can be cleaned using a damp cloth. Always dry with a clean cloth after wiping.

The bracket is normally used in the form of an inverted "L". To use, simply hold the long side of the bracket, and gently unscrew the thumb nut to allow the smaller inner "L" bracket to be moved along the slot of the outer "L" bracket.

The inner "L" bracket is then placed between the two cake boards. Tighten the thumb nut when the desired depth is obtained. Insert other brackets to achieve the same depth. The floating bridge lines for single or tiered extension work can then be supported and linked together. The bracket when fully extended will support a floating collar or suspended floating collar as featured in the 'True Love'. The bracket can easily be removed by unscrewing the thumb nut. Then slide the bracket away from the cake board.

The Cake

Whatever form of decorative technique you intend to use it is very important to have a good base on which to work. I find that sponge or fruit cakes make perfect bases. You can add many extra ingredients to make a sponge cake more interesting, for example coconut, cherries, chocolate, etc. In my experience a bride will often ask for a sponge top tier and it is a pleasure to be able to offer something different from the normal sponge type of cake. Always remember, your finished work will form the centre-piece of the occasion for which it has been made and a few minutes of extra care during preparation will make all the difference to the finished creation.

There are several good quality cake recipes you can use and I have included two of my own favourites.

Before making the cake it will be necessary for you to line your cake tin neatly thus enabling you to work on a cake which is as smooth as possible.

Lining the cake tin

1. Cut two lengths of greaseproof paper long enough to make a double sided lining which will fit inside your cake tin.

2. Cut two sheets of greaseproof paper slightly smaller and the same shape as the base of your cake tin.

3. Cover the base and sides of your cake tin with a little oil.

4. Place the two sheets of greaseproof paper cut at step 2 into the bottom of your tin making sure you oil between each sheet.

5. Place the greaseproof paper lining cut in step 1 into your cake tin, ensuring that the paper does not overlap the base. Grease between each sheet. (see figure 1)

6. Place a collar of newspaper around the outside of your cake tin if wished.

The rich fruit cake recipe

This makes a good quality fruit cake suitable for most occasions. It needs about three weeks to mature after baking, before it is ready to cover with Marzipan and Sugarpaste. If you intend to make a tiered wedding cake you will need to ensure that the bottom, middle and top tiers are graduated in depth, the bottom being the deepest. For the purposes of extension work I like my bottom tier to be about 75mm (3") deep, the middle 70mm (2¾") and the top 62mm (2½") before they are covered. It is therefore a good idea to line all your cake tins at once and fill your bottom and middle tier tins with cake mixture at the same time, thus enabling you to achieve this difference in depth.

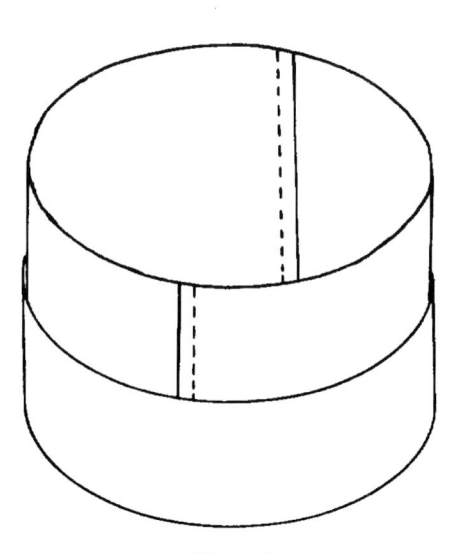

Figure 1

The recipe given below is for an 200mm (8") round or 175mm (7") square cake. A table of quantities needed for alternative shapes and sizes is given at the end of the book.

Ingredients for an 200mm (8") round, or 175mm (7") square cake.

Use **all** metric or **all** imperial measurements throughout the recipe.

225gms (8oz)	caster sugar
225gms (8oz)	butter
280gms (10oz)	s.r.flour
28gms (1oz)	ground almonds
28gms (1oz)	chopped blanched almonds
225gms (8oz)	currants
225gms (8oz)	sultanas
168gms (6oz)	raisins
56gms (2oz)	mixed peel
56gms (2oz)	glacé cherries cut into quarters
20mls (1 Tbsp)	milk

4 Eggs (size 2)
¼ Tsp nutmeg
½ Tsp mixed spice
1 Tbsp treacle
½ wineglass brandy
¼ lemon rind finely grated

Method

Place the fruit into a bowl and rinse well. Dry by placing on Kitchen paper and replace in the bowl, then pour in the brandy.

Cover with a clean tea towel and leave overnight in a cool dry place.

Cream the butter, sugar, treacle, spice, nutmeg and lemon rind until light and fluffy.

Beat in the eggs, checking each is fresh by breaking it into a cup before adding to the main cake mixture.

Stir in the milk.

Stir in half of the flour. Mix well.

Stir in the second half of the flour. Mix well.

Stir in the glace cherries, mixed peel, chopped almonds and fruit and brandy mixture.

Turn into the greased, lined cake tin and cover the top of the tin. (see figure 2) Do not allow the cake mixture to come into contact with the covering paper. Bake in the centre of a pre-heated oven for about three hours at gas mark 2, 150°C, 300°F. Do not remove the covering paper until the top of the cake is a light golden brown. This will take approximately 2 hours.

To test if the cake is cooked insert a skewer into its centre. If it comes out clean and the cake is golden brown it is cooked. If not leave the cake in the oven for another 10 to 15 minutes and test again.

Before removing the cake from the oven read the section on preparation of the cake for covering.

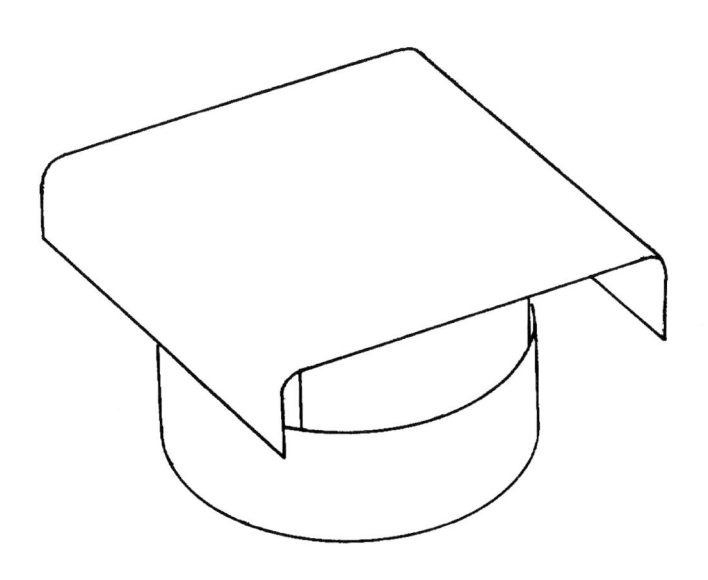

Figure 2

Handy Tip

If the mixture begins to curdle add approximately two tablespoons of the flour to the mixture before continuing to add the eggs.

Sponge cake

The recipe given below is for an 200mm (8") round or 175mm (7") square cake.

A table of quantities needed for alternative shapes and sizes is given at the end of the book.

Ingredients for an 200mm (8") round, or 175mm (7") square.
450gms (16oz) caster sugar.
450gms (16oz) margarine.
450gms (16oz) s. r. flour.
1 dessert sp. warm water.
8 eggs (size 2).

Method

Cream together the sugar, margarine and warm water until light and fluffy.

Beat in the eggs checking each is fresh by breaking it into a cup before adding to the cake mixture.

Gently stir in the flour. Do not fold it in.

Turn into the greased, lined cake tin and place a piece of greaseproof paper over the top of the tin. Bake in the centre of an oven for approximately one hour at gas mark 4, 180°C, 350°F, removing the paper from the top of the cake after 30 minutes. To test if the cake is cooked gently press the centre of the cake and see if it springs back into its original shape. The colour should be golden brown and a skewer inserted into its centre should come out clean. Do not attempt to remove the cake from the oven until all of the above tests have proved successful. If the cake appears to be burning on the surface but is not cooked in the centre turn the oven down slightly.

Preparation of the cake for covering

The cake needs to be as even and crease free as possible to be in an ideal state for covering. Dents, crease marks, etc. are extremely difficult to remove when you come to Marzipan/Sugarpaste the cake, so a little time spent when removing the cake from the oven will make life a lot easier when you come to covering.

Turn the cake out of the cake tin onto a wire rack. Then immediately turn the cake back onto a flat surface. This ensures the base of the cake remains as even as possible for covering. (see figure 3)

Never leave a cake on a wire rack to cool. Any impressions left on the base of the cake will make it very difficult to obtain a very flat surface so essential if a good finish is to be achieved.

Storage of cakes

Wherever possible store fruit cakes in their original paper coverings in clean, dry, conditions. Double wrap the cake in greaseproof and store in a cake box or place on a flat surface covered with a cake tin. DO NOT SEAL THE TIN. Air should always be able to circulate around the wrapped cake at all times. If desired 1 dessert spoon of brandy may be added to the cake every two weeks.

I do not recommend storing a fruit cake for more than six weeks unless covered with marzipan and sugarpaste. Once covered, the cake should keep for about six months if necessary. Do not store sponge cakes. Cover and decorate as soon as they are cold.

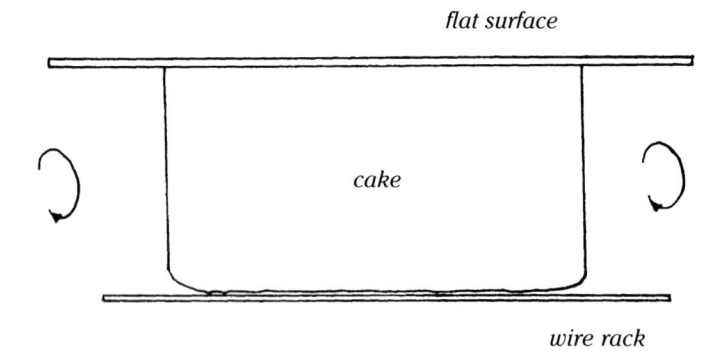

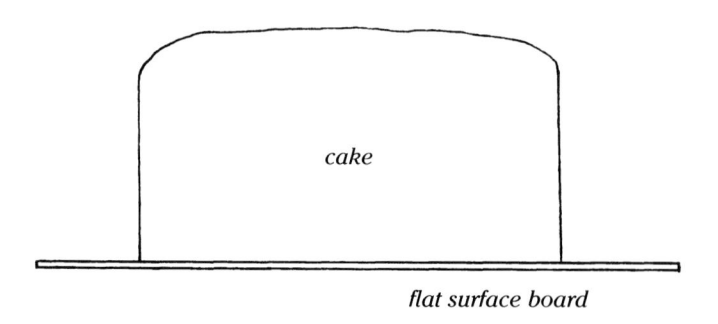

Figure 3

Royal Icing

Royal icing is made by beating together icing sugar and egg white. During this process millions of air bubbles become incorporated into the icing. When ready the icing should stand up in peaks.

Either pure egg albumen, egg white or substitute albumen may be used in making royal icing. Pure egg white may be used in the ratio of one egg white to 225gms (8oz) icing sugar. Always ensure it is separated properly and that no yolk is present. Albumen powder should always be stored in an airtight container and remember to label all containers clearly.

Substitute albumen and albumen powder can be more economical to use as there are no problems with trying to find a use for left over egg yolks.

This may seem a minor inconvenience until you attempt to cover a three tier wedding cake and discover you need several eggs.

When making royal icing it is essential that all your equipment is totally grease free. To do this add 1 teaspoon salt to your mixing bowl and rub this around the bowl. Rinse in boiling water then leave to air-dry. Always use a clean wooden spoon kept specially for this purpose.

Given below are three recipes for making royal icing, one for each type of albumen. Egg white and pure albumen powder make the strongest royal icing most suitable for filigree work. I tend to use substitute albumen icing for most of my work including extension work and have had very little trouble with breakages.

(1) Using egg white

Use one size 2 egg white to 225gms (8oz) sifted icing sugar.

Place the sifted icing sugar into a clean, grease free bowl and add the egg white. Using a wooden spoon kept exclusively for this purpose beat the mixture slowly. At this stage the icing will seem very heavy and shiny. Continue to beat the mixture until it forms little peaks when the spoon is removed and the icing has lost its shine; (see plate 1) this may take up to twenty minutes of continuous beating. You see why I said to beat it slowly. In my experience beating fast does not seem to speed up the process very much and only makes you too tired to continue. Cover the icing with a damp cloth or place into a clean, grease free, glass bowl in an airtight container to store until required.

Plate 1- Egg White

(2) Substitute albumen powder

Place 450gms (1lb) sifted icing sugar into a clean, grease free bowl and add one rounded tablespoon of substitute albumen powder and three tablespoons of warm water. Repeat beating procedure as for recipe (1) until the icing stands up in peaks. This procedure may take a little less than twenty minutes depending on how hard you beat the icing. Do not beat it too hard. (see plate 2)

If you have a food mixer it is possible to make the icing in this. Follow your chosen recipe procedure as above substituting the machine to do your beating for you. Always set your machine to its lowest setting and do not leave the icing to be beaten for more than four minutes as too much air will become incorporated into it.

(3) Pure albumen powder

Place three and one half level 5ml teaspoons of pure albumen powder into a cup and add seven teaspoons of cold water. Leave this overnight to combine. Sieve before using. Sieve 225gms (8oz) icing sugar into a clean, grease free bowl and add the sieved albumen mixture. Repeat the beating procedure as above until the icing stands up in soft peaks. This takes about 20 minutes. Note: This icing tends to be a little softer when making than recipe (1) and when finished the peaks have a tendency to flop over at the top (see plate 1).

Adding colour to royal icing

Care must be taken when adding colour to your icing. Always add colour when the icing is at peaking consistency, ensuring the colour you achieve is at least two shades lighter than you will eventually need. The coloured icing will darken for at least twenty minutes before attaining its final shade. (see plate 3)

This is known as "wetting out".

All food colours, when added to royal icing display this property over a period of time. Therefore always make enough coloured icing to complete the task in hand as it is very difficult to match colours later.

As a guide I always make up at least 680gms (1½lb) of the deepest shade of coloured royal icing for a single tiered cake with double extension work on a coloured bridge.

Plate 2 - Substitute albumen powder

Plate 3 - Colouring Royal Icing

Covering with Marzipan

When decorating a cake with extension work it is important that the sides of the sugarpaste cake are as straight and smooth as possible. I have often been asked how this finish can be obtained and have tried to make my instructions as clear as I can in order that you may be able to achieve a similar effect. Throughout the text you will find that I refer to different areas of the hand with which to perform various smoothing actions. In all cases I have used a letter code, a reference for which is included at the end of this section. The method I use is suitable for covering any shape of cake.

The instructions given are in numbered stages for easy reference, thus allowing you to progress through each step in a logical way.

A table of quantities necessary to cover various shapes and sizes of cake can also be found on page 16, covering with sugarpaste.

1. Turn the cake upside down and place on a cake board at least 75mm (3") larger than the cake. This protects your delicate work and makes it easier to transport.

For example an 200mm (8") cake should be placed on an 275mm (11") board etc., if it is to be a single tier. This allows 38mm (1½") on all sides of the cake and once marzipan and/or sugarpaste have been added, together with your side decoration leaves a border of 12mm (½") around the cake.

If you find that the gap between the side of your cake and the board is greater than 12mm (½") remove the cake and cut off some of its top. (see figure 1)

To do this place it back into its original cake tin and raise it using a firm support, an unused cake board is ideal for this. Make sure the central portion which needs to be removed appears above the side of the tin. Using a bread knife cut off this excess, the top of the cake tin is thus used as a level to ensure that your cut is straight and even. (see figure 2)

2. Fix the cake to the board with about five small dabs of royal icing spaced evenly around the centre. Always ensure that the cake is in the centre of the board and that there is an even area of board around the outside edge of the cake.

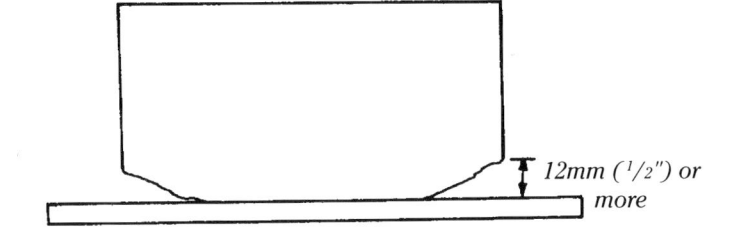

12mm (½") or more

Figure 1

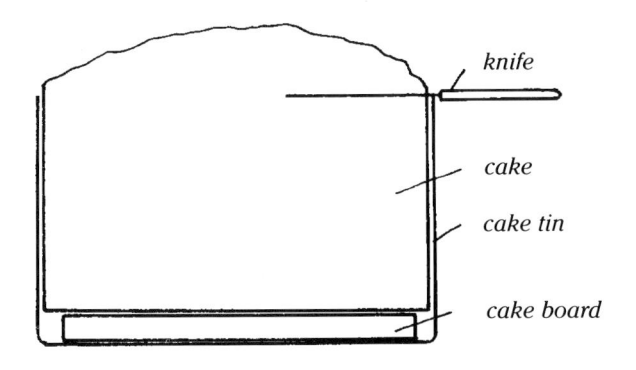

knife
cake
cake tin
cake board

Figure 2

3. Thinly brush the surface of the cake with boiled Apricot jam. Fill in any cracks, dents, etc. with marzipan making sure you smooth the surface until it is as near perfect as possible. Take some marzipan and roll into a sausage shape. Place a spirit level on top of the cake and gently push the sausage of marzipan into any gaps around the base of the cake where it meets the cake board. (see figure 3) Cut off any excess with a knife making sure the top of the cake is level. If too high remove some of the sausage if too low add some more.

4. Take a knife and hold it vertical to your cake side. Gently move the knife around the cake cutting off any excess marzipan and keeping the side as straight as possible. (see figure 4) Cover the marzipan with Apricot jam.

5. Place one tablespoon of icing sugar into a piece of butter muslin and tie up the corners to make a bag. Use this to dust your work surface. Then take sufficient marzipan (see the table of quantities at the end of the book) to cover your cake. Knead this into a ball ensuring that any cracks are kneaded beneath the ball and the top is smooth.

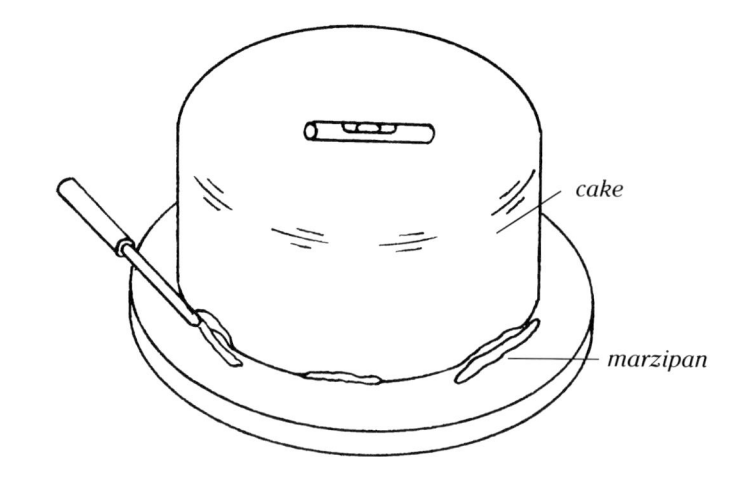

Figure 3

> ### Handy Tip
> Never use cornflour when rolling out your marzipan or sugarpaste as this may create problems which may not be evident until the decorated cake is cut.

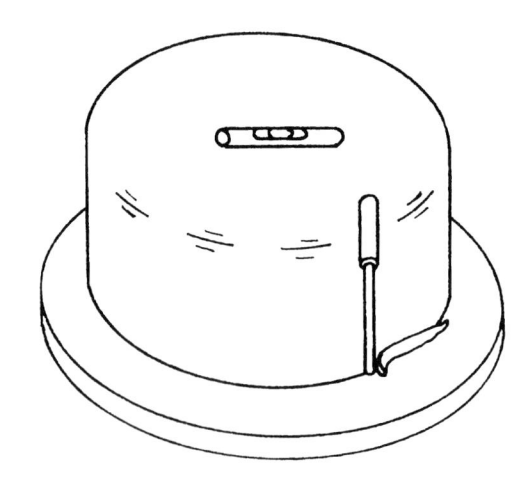

Figure 4

6. Roll out, turning frequently and adding more sifted icing sugar to the work surface as necessary to prevent sticking. Measure the cake allowing 12mm ($\frac{1}{2}$") extra on each side. (see figure 5)

7. Measure the marzipan and continue rolling it out until it is the same size as the measured cake. Then using your right hand, quickly flick the rolling pin towards you, lifting the marzipan with your left hand. Drop the marzipan over the rolling pin.

> ### Handy Tip
> I find it helps to raise the cake a few inches above your work surface before completing this step. This gives a good all round working height and makes it easier to turn when this becomes necessary.

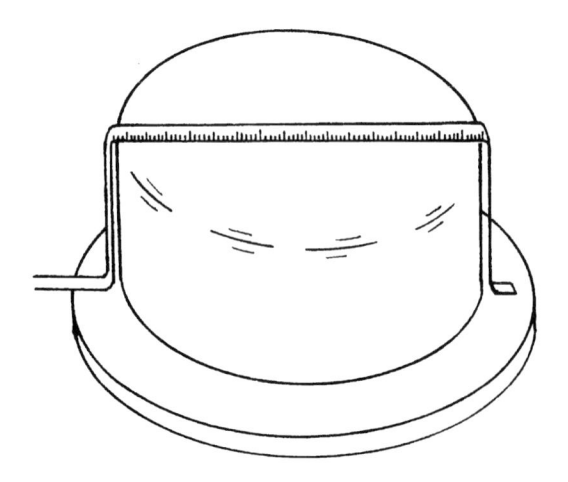

Figure 5

8. Work the rolling pin underneath the marzipan until it is in the centre. Lift the rolling pin and gently place the edge of the marzipan farthest from you over the top of the cake so that it lies against the cake side with 12mm (½") extra resting on the cake board. (see figure 6)

9. Gently drape the rest of the marzipan over the cake by unrolling it towards you.

10. Lift the overlapping edge of the marzipan from the cake board and using the side of the hand (see figure 7 marked B), gently smooth it over the top edge and down the side.

Try to preserve the curve on the top edge of the cake by gently cupping the side of your hand around this edge and rolling it backwards and forwards whilst flattening the top of the cake with the palm of your other hand. (see figure 8)

Any air bubbles can be removed by gently pricking with a sterilised fine pointed needle. The surface may then be gently smoothed once more to remove the pin hole.

11. Gradually bring the sides of your hands (Fig 7 marked A) over the opposite sides of the cake and smooth the marzipan taking care not to create any dents or ridges. This is particularly important around the bottom edge.

12. Take a round bladed knife and cut away the excess marzipan to within 12mm (½") of the base of the cake. (see figure 9)

13. Using the flat side of the knife gently pat the remaining 12mm (½") into the cake side. If a ridge begins to form, cut off the excess and ensure the cake sides are straight. (see figure 10)

14. Gently smooth down the opposite sides of the cake using the palms and sides of your hands, turning the cake as you do so, thus achieving as smooth a surface as possible.

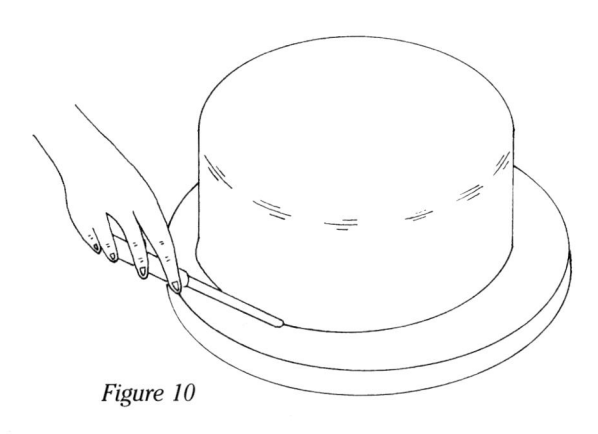

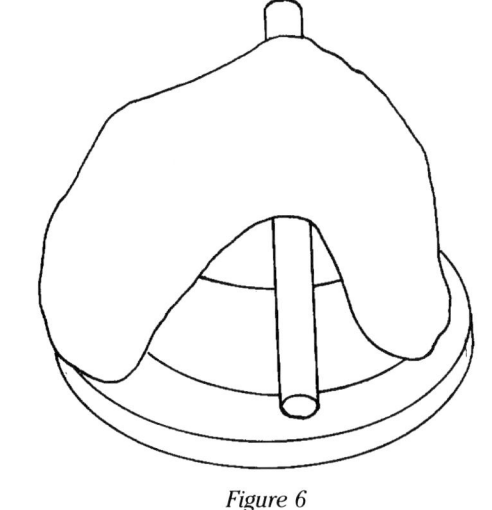

Figure 6

Figure 7

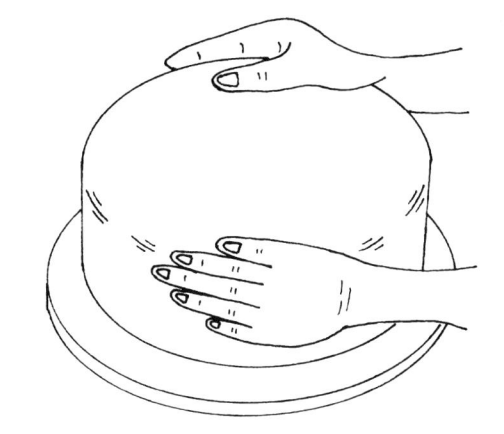

Figure 8

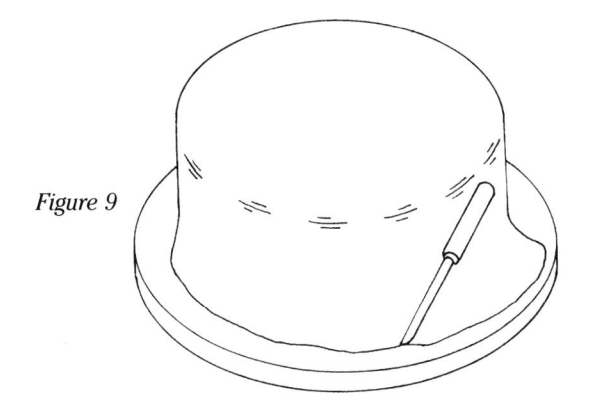

Figure 9

Figure 10

Covering with Sugarpaste

Sugarpaste is a very versatile form of cake covering which never really sets hard. It can be used to cover almost any shape of cake, producing a smooth, even finish which can be easily cut with a knife. Available commercially from sugarcraft shops and larger supermarkets, some brands tend to be softer than others. I would therefore suggest you experiment by using a small quantity of each until you find one with which you feel confident. Any unused sugarpaste can always be moulded into flowers, animals, etc., or if a little Peppermint oil is added, make very tasty Peppermint creams. You can of course make your own sugarpaste quite easily. Just follow the recipe.

Sugarpaste

Ingredients

450gms (1lb) icing sugar

1 egg white

2 Tbsp liquid glucose

1. Place the egg white and liquid glucose into a bowl and sift in half the icing sugar.
2. Mix with a clean wooden spoon adding more sifted icing sugar until it is all thoroughly combined.
3. Using your fingers, form the mixture into a ball and turn out onto a work surface lightly dusted with icing sugar.
4. Knead thoroughly until completely smooth and silky.
5. Place the sugarpaste into a plastic bag and remove as much air as possible.

> **Handy tip**
> Always keep any unused sugarpaste in an airtight bag.

If the outer edge of the sugarpaste becomes dry and hard, cut this away before using. Sometimes the dry pieces can be saved for use if they are first kneaded with a little water until they re-form into a smooth, silky ball.

Colouring sugarpaste

It is possible to colour sugarpaste very successfully. Add your colour in small quantities, a smear of paste or a drop of liquid from a cocktail stick dipped into the colour are ideal. Spread the colour over the sugarpaste and knead it until it is thoroughly mixed. There should be no streaks visible when the sugarpaste has been rolled out. To cover a three tiered wedding cake with coloured sugarpaste, always colour enough paste to complete the task. It is extremely difficult to match colours at a later stage if you find you have not coloured enough.

> **Handy tip**
> Cut the kneaded paste in half and examine. If you can see streaks of colour knead again.

Use this table for marzipan and sugarpaste. The quantities stated should be sufficient to cover the top and sides of the cake in one piece.

The depth of the cake should not exceed 76mm (3"). Always add 112grms.(1/4 lb) extra marzipan for filling in any dents, cracks, etc., in the cake. For a large cake in excess of 200mm (8") add 225grms.(1/2 lb) for filling. Remember, if you are only using sugarpaste to cover the cake, use sugarpaste as your filling in place of marzipan.

Shape	Size							
square, octagon hexagon, petal	- -	150mm 6"	175mm 7"	200mm 8"	225mm 9"	250mm 10"	275mm 11"	300mm 12"
round, heart, oval	150mm 6"	175mm 7"	200mm 8"	225mm 9"	250mm 10"	275mm 11"	300mm 12"	- -
quantity required	392gms 14oz	562gms 1lb 4oz	730gms 1lb10oz	842gms 1lb 14oz	1236gms 2lb 12oz	1462gms 3lb 4oz	1603gms 3lb 9oz	1856gms 4lb 2oz

Heart's Delight

Christmas Time

Christmas Time by Gill Martin took first place in the Novice Sugarpaste at the London Christmas Exhibition 1989

Covering the Cake

Fruit and sponge cakes are both suitable for covering with sugarpaste and do not need to be covered with marzipan first.

However I always use a slightly thicker layer of sugarpaste on cakes that have not been covered with marzipan as this produces a more even finish.

The method for covering a cake with sugarpaste is very similar to that used when covering with marzipan and is described below. If you do not wish to marzipan your cake before covering it with sugarpaste follow steps 1-4 covering with marzipan substituting sugarpaste for marzipan in the text. Then continue as below beginning at step 2.

1. Measure the marzipan covered cake allowing 12mm ($^1/_2$") extra on each side. Brush the cake with water or alcohol (e.g. Brandy, Whisky). (see figure 1)

2. Dust the work surface with icing sugar. Take sufficient sugarpaste (see table of quantities for marzipan and use the same quantities as shown) and knead into a ball. Ensure any creases are underneath and the top is smooth and crease free.

3. Roll out the sugarpaste until it is the same size as the measured cake. Using your right hand flick the rolling pin towards you, lifting the sugarpaste with your left hand. Drop the sugarpaste over the rolling pin.

4. Place the sugarpaste over the cake starting with a 12mm ($^1/_2$") overlap at the back and bringing the sugarpaste over the cake by unrolling the rolling pin towards you. (see figure 2)

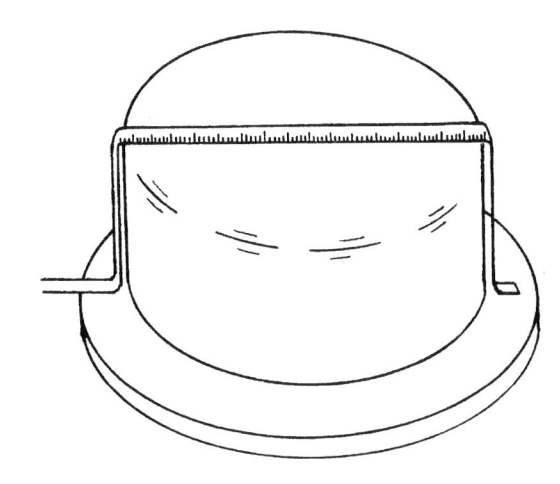

Figure 1

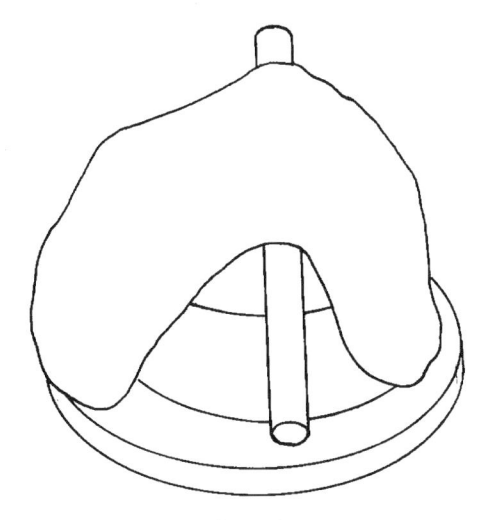

Figure 2

Handy Tip
As with the marzipan cake covering it is easier to have your cake raised a few inches above the work surface before you attempt the above stage.

Do not worry if the sugarpaste breaks when you lift it. You can always roll it up and begin again. This is not possible if you roll out on cornflour as it dries the sugarpaste too quickly and cannot be kneaded into the sugarpaste very successfully.

If you find that the sugarpaste does not quite fit the cake, don't worry, use the palm of your hand to stretch this on top of the cake towards the side that is not quite covered. Continue to draw this excess down the cake side using your fingers and smoothing round the side until the uncovered area is covered down to the cake board.

5. Smooth the cake top, gently pricking any air bubbles and smoothing out the pin holes with the palm of the hand. (see figure 3 marked B)

6. Gradually work your hands over the opposite cake sides, curving your fingers (see figure 3 marked C) around the top edge, thus rounding it as much as possible. (see figure 4)

7. Smooth the cake sides using the areas of the hand (see figure 3 marked C) then cut off the excess with a round bladed knife leaving about 6mm ($1/4$") overlapping the board. (see figure 5) Gently pat this into the cake side ensuring you do not have a ridge. (see figure 6)

Handy Tip

Do not let water come into contact with the sugarpaste surface as this will cause damage. Always wash and dry your hands thoroughly then rub them with a little icing sugar before smoothing the cake.

A shine on the sugarpaste is desirable and is created by the smoothing actions of your hands. You may choose to use a piece of silk to shine the cake if you wish. Personally I have never felt the need to do this.

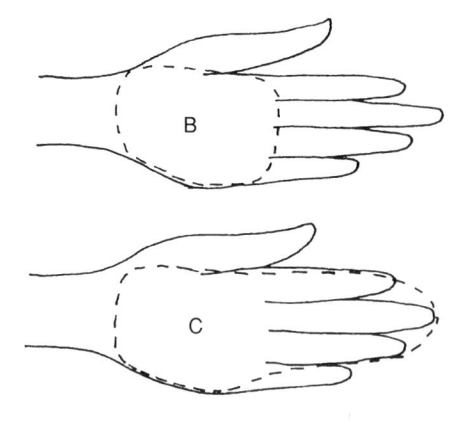

Figure 3

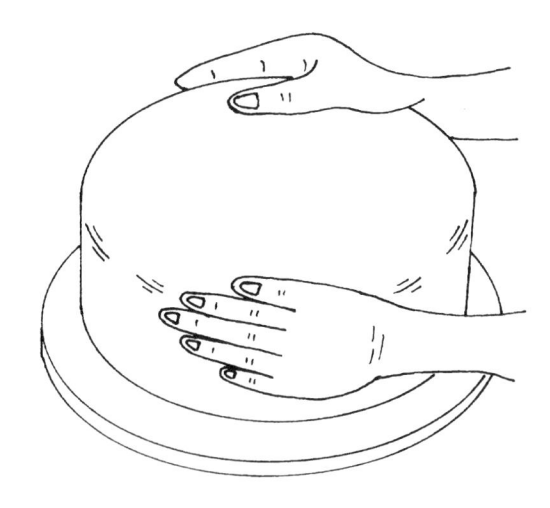

Figure 4

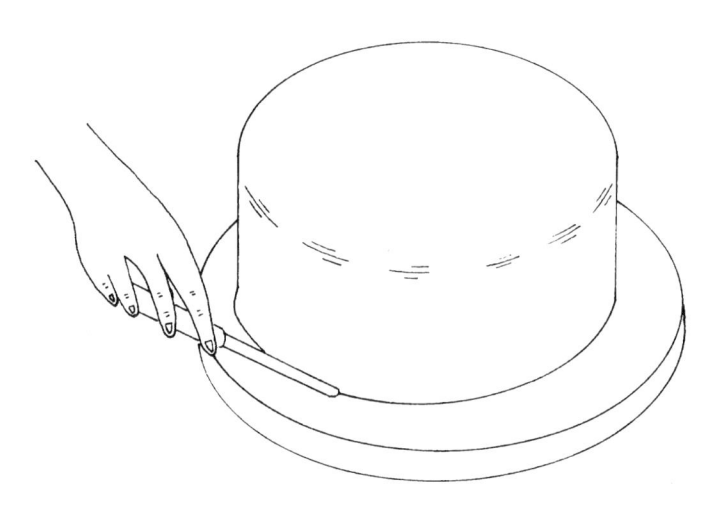

Figure 6

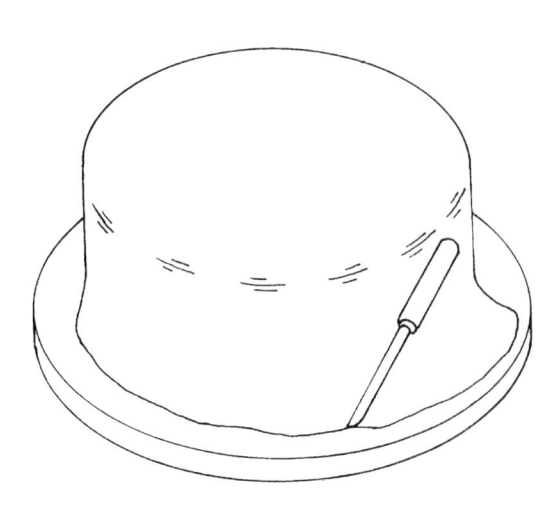

Figure 5

Pattern making

Before beginning to pipe extension work onto a cake you will need to follow a pattern. Making paper patterns need not be a daunting experience if you follow the steps below. The instructions given are for a round or oval cake. If you are intending to make patterns for another shape, work on one side at a time following the procedure below but omitting any folding of the paper.

Pattern making for fixed extension work

1. Using a piece of adding machine roll at least 37mm (1½") wide measure round the side of your cake. Mark the adding machine roll with a pencil where the paper meets. Add approximately 6mm (¼") and cut off the end. (see figure 1)

2. Fold in the 6mm (¼") extra and then fold the paper over twice. This will give you four quarters when the paper is unfolded. Fold four times for sixteen sections, etc. The number of folds you make will depend on the number of sections you want.

3. Keeping the paper folded, mark the centre of one section, A, B.

4. Mark about 6mm (¼") above points C,D on both sides E,F. Join with a curve the centre of which should pass through point B. I usually hunt round the Kitchen for a cup or glass to do this, using the rim as my curve. (see figure 2)

5. Hold the paper tightly, ensuring all the sections are lined up and cut off the paper along the curve. Discard the bottom, shaded section. (see figure 3)

Figure 1

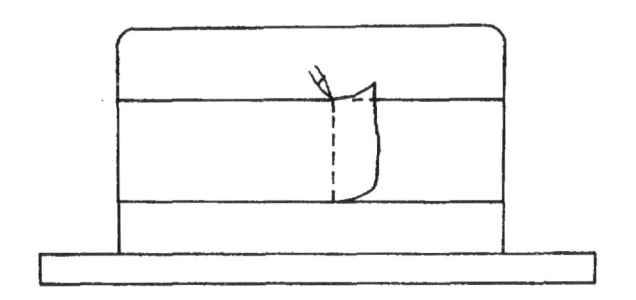

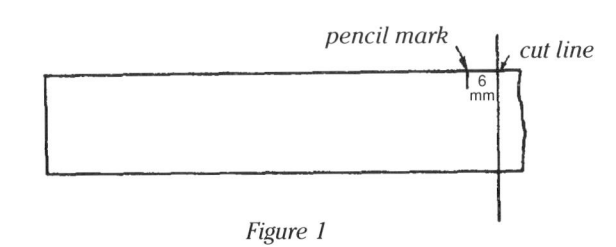

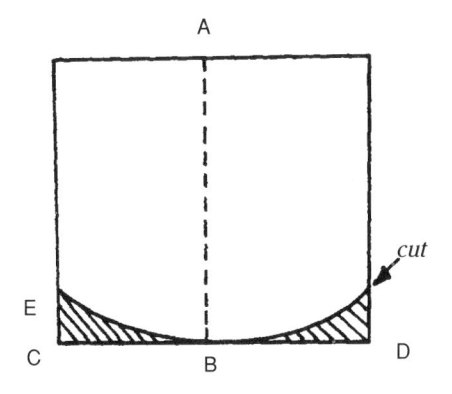

Figure 3

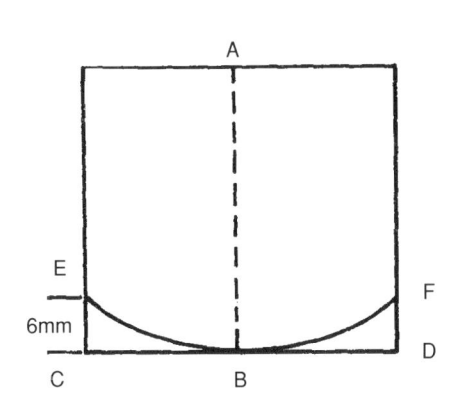

Figure 2

6. Open out and iron the pattern flat.

7. Join the ends of the pattern using the 6mm (¼") flap to ensure a good fit. (see figure 4)

8. Gently ease this collar over the top and down the sides of the cake. (see figure 5)

> ### *Handy Tip*
> If working on a square, hexagon, octagon or heart, work on one side at a time.

9. If the collar does not quite fit. Break it into four quarters and leave a small gap between each quarter when marking the pattern onto the cake. (see figure 6)

Figure 4

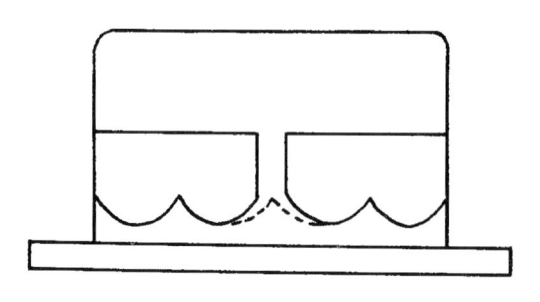

Figure 6

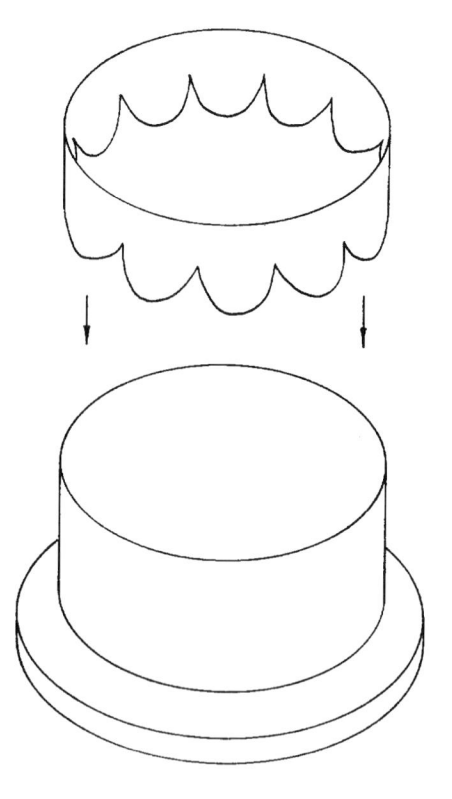

Figure 5

10. Check the pattern is level down the cake sides. Use a ruler to level the sides, adding pins just below the points of the curves when measured. The pattern is then eased onto these and the points of the curves are marked onto the cake sides with another pin. (See figure 7)

11. Move the collar upward about 25-31mm (1-1¼") above the bottom curve. Check the pattern is level and line up the top and bottom curves as shown. Score around the top curve. (see figure 8)

12. If a different shaped top is desired, remove the paper collar from the cake and refold. Draw the shape you require and cut accordingly. (see figure 9)

13. Score this shaped top onto the cake following steps 7-10 but omitting the scoring in step 9. (see figure 10)

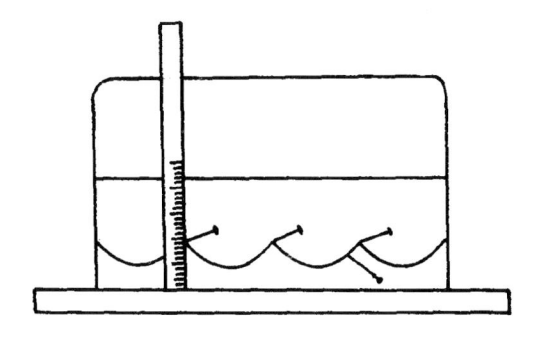

figure 7

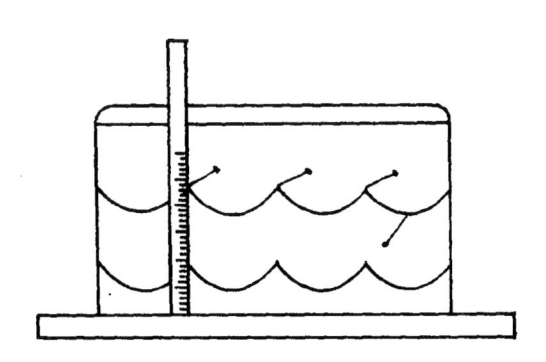

figure 8

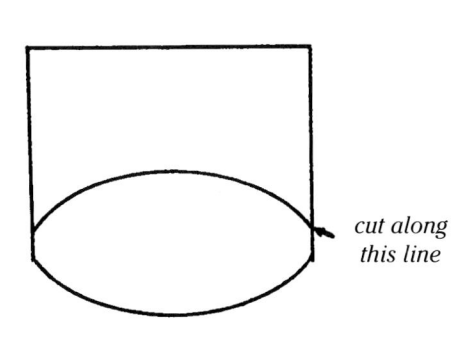

Figure 9

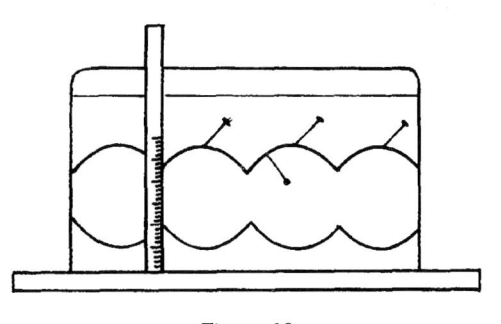

cut along this line

Figure 10

Pattern making for floating extension work

When working with floating extension work it is necessary to make two patterns, one for the cake side and another for the floating bridge line onto which you will pipe your dropped strings.

Side pattern

Complete steps 1-8 as described in the section working on a fixed bridge. If at this point the collar does not quite fit, break it into four quarters. Leave a small gap between each quarter when marking the pattern onto the cake. (see figure 1)

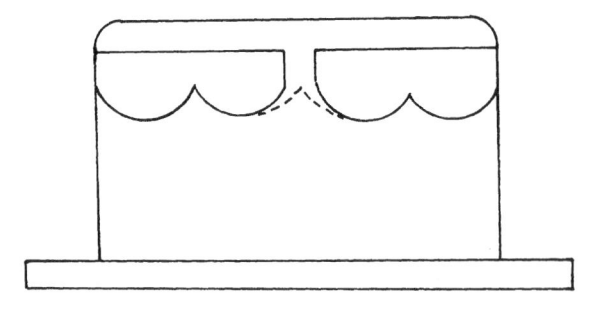

Figure 1

Floating bridge pattern

1. Measure the diameter of the cake and divide by two. Using a pair of compasses opened to this size, draw a circle onto a sheet of paper. The circle should be the same size as your cake. Mark this circle c/l (cake line).

2. Draw another circle over the cake line 25mm (1") larger. Mark this circle f.

3. Draw another circle over the second line f. 12mm (½") larger. Mark this circle s. (see figure 2)

4. Divide the circles into two. Using a protractor divide the circle into 4, 8 and so on. (see figure 3)

Handy tip

I usually find I use 16 or 24 divisions to work on. This makes curves which are not too deep or wide and fit in very well with most side designs.

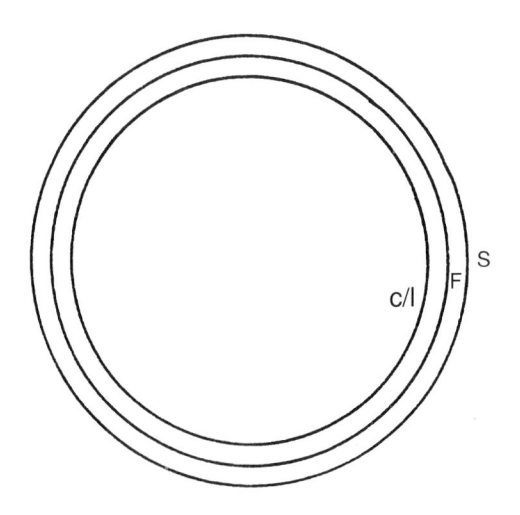

Figure 2

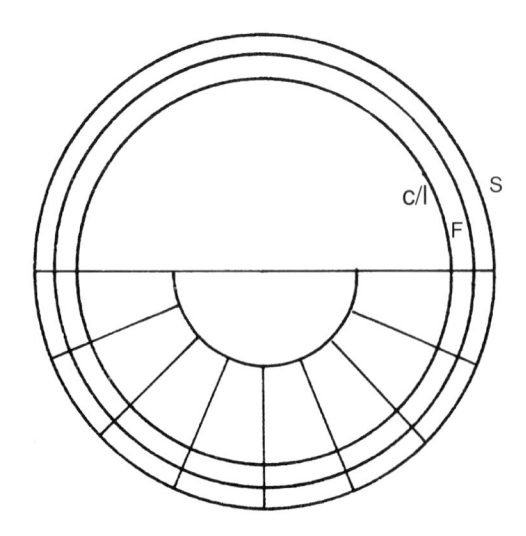

Figure 3

5. Using one segment, find the centre by drawing a straight line connecting points A and B where the curve touches each side of the segment. Measure this line and divide in half. Mark this halfway point C. (see figure 4)

6. Draw a straight line passing through point C from the point D. Repeat steps 5 and 6 until all the segments have been divided.

7. Inscribe a curve between points A and B the centre of which should just touch point E (see figure 5) Repeat with all the segments. (see figure 6) Cut the circle in half and then cut along half circles against the base of the cake and adjust if necessary until they fit. This may mean cutting the sections into half again and leaving a small gap between each. (see figure 7)

Handy tip

Always ensure that your bridge line curves match in with the pattern for the cake side. For example two bridge curves equal one side curve, there are an equal number of side and bridge curves, etc. This will make lining up the side and bridge line easier.

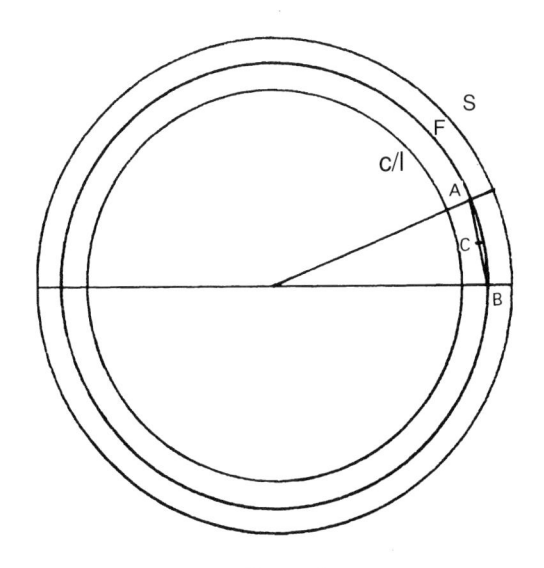

Figure 4

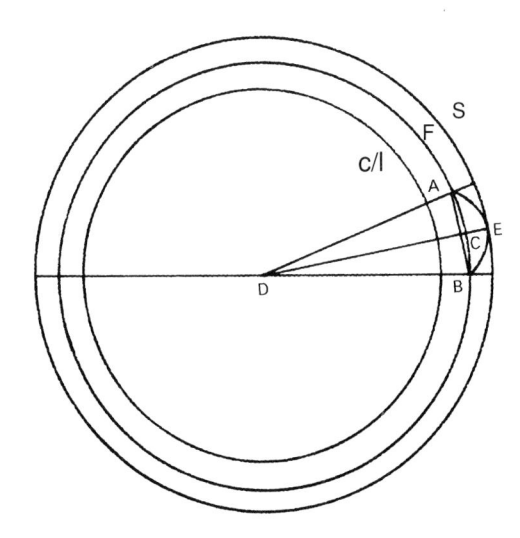

Figure 5

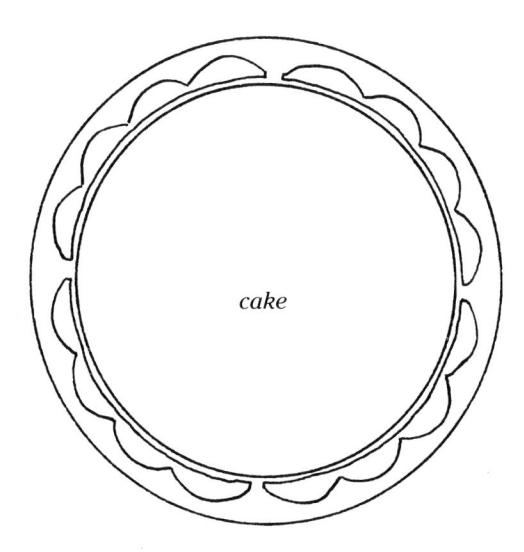

Figure 7

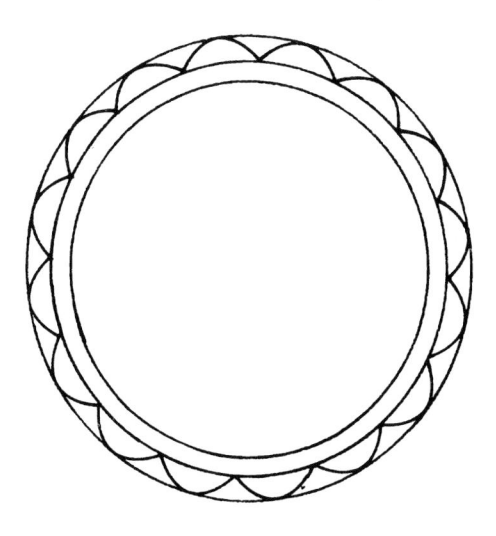

Figure 6

Ribbon Insertion

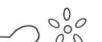

This technique must always be applied to a cake freshly covered with sugarpaste. It looks very attractive when combined with embroidery and extension work or on the top of a cake framing a picture. It is not a difficult technique to master. Before you begin to apply this technique you will need a pattern.

The pattern used for marking the top of your extension work is also used as the basis for your ribbon insertion pattern.

Using one of the curves from your extension work side pattern, mark the centre point.

Take your ribbon insertion tool and mark the pattern. The number of ribbon inserts will depend on the width of the curved section. (see figures 1 and 2) For example a small curve may only take three inserts one in the centre with one on each side. On a larger curve the ribbon inserts tend to look more attractive if set on either side of the centre line.

1. Mark your chosen pattern onto the cake (see figure 3) and prick the ribbon insertion points with a pin. Always ensure that your pattern is positioned correctly before marking the cake.

2. Push the ribbon insertion tool into the sugarpaste together with a short length of ribbon. Once in place carefully remove the tool.

If your tool has two prongs hold the ribbon in place with a pin and gradually withdraw the tool. (see figure 4) The ribbon should stay in place. If you do not have such a tool follow step 3 below.

3. Hold the ribbon inserted in the cake with a pin and gently push the free end into the second marked section using the ribbon insertion tool or your finger. (see figure 5)

Figure 1

Figure 2

Figure 3

Figure 4

Figure 5

Handy Tip

The ribbon should stand out about 3mm ($1/8$") from the cake's side to its centre. Once you have a piece of ribbon inserted to the correct depth remove it and use it as a guide to cut the remaining lengths of ribbon you will require. One piece of ribbon will be needed for every insertion of the ribbon insertion tool.

Continue to insert ribbon until the pattern is finished. Decorate the ribbon with embroidery to finish. There are many different applications for ribbon insertion. For example Golden Showers page 52 and Best of Friends page 35.

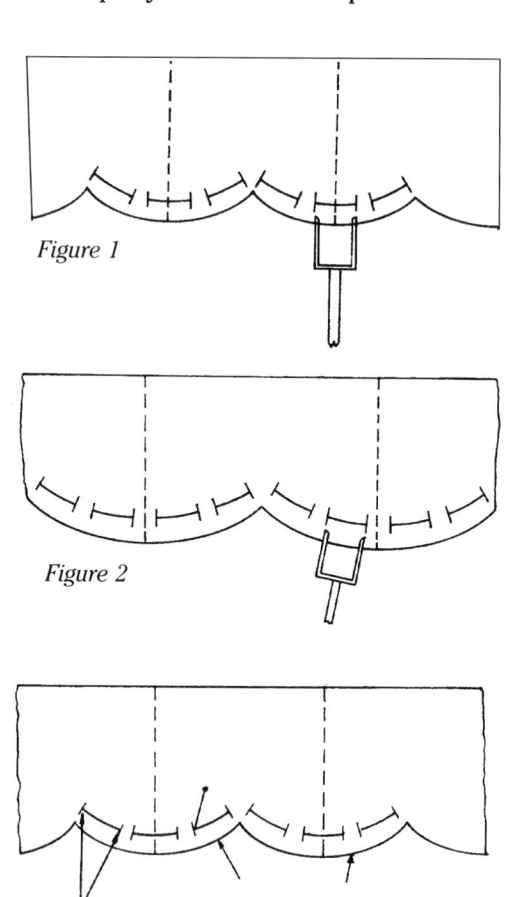

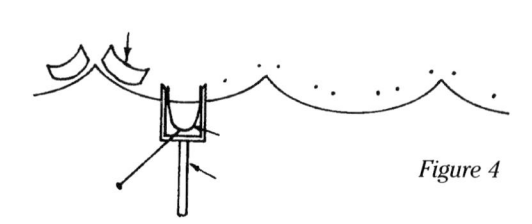

Useful Piping Techniques

To decorate any cake you will probably require piping at some stage, whether it be writing, embroidery or the more delicate forms of filigree, lace and extension work.

It is therefore important that you understand the different techniques necessary to enable you to pipe any design you may need.

By following each of the piping exercises step by step and practising until you can accomplish any of them with ease, you should be ready to tackle any design featured in this book.

Before you begin piping with royal icing it is necessary for you to bring it to peaking consistency. Place some icing from your storage container into a grease free cup and stir with a knife until it stands up in peaks when the knife is removed. It is also very important that you understand the significance of having a different consistency for each piping technique you may use.

Consistency of royal icing for piping

Royal icing when used for piped work needs to be carefully prepared each time it is used. This is especially true for extension work where you are working with very fine tubes and the icing does not always flow easily. Correct consistency is very important and I have tried to explain as clearly as possible how to achieve this.

When piping fine lines, extension work, etc using a no. 0, 00 tube it is sometimes necessary to sieve your icing through butter muslin before you begin. This removes lumps, large particles of sugar, etc. If the icing is hard to sieve it is the wrong consistency and needs to be softened and beaten a little more before re-sieving. It should then pass through easily.

Before you begin piping, always test if your icing is of the correct consistency. This will largely depend on the use to which the icing is put e.g. for extension work drop strings, the icing will need to be softer than for fine flat lines. To test, place a little icing into a piping bag fitted with the appropriate tube. Pipe a small amount of icing from the tube. If it does not flow smoothly and requires a great deal of effort to pipe, it is too stiff. Soften it with a little water and repeat. Ideally the icing should be just soft enough to pipe through the tube when continuous pressure is placed on the bag. You should feel no discomfort when piping unless you suffer from arthritis in which case you may need to soften the icing a little more.

Greaseproof piping bags

Many people are unsure how to make greaseproof piping bags correctly and so resort to commercially made bags instead. I have to admit I used to be one of these people until I learned how easy it is to make bags correctly. You will find that if you want to pipe beautiful, delicate extension work, greaseproof bags are a must. They are versatile, light to handle and you have a great deal of control over the flow of icing. This is most important. You will also find that you need to use far less icing per bag than with many commercially made ones. This enables you to use several bags at a time, which, when working with floating extension work, is a great asset. Once you have mastered making bags you will never want to return to commercially made bags again so, please, if you find this technique difficult at first, keep trying, I did and have never looked back.

1. Take a piece of greaseproof paper and fold along the diagonal corners. Cut along the folded line. (see figure 1)

2. Hold the paper up by putting the corner marked (A) between the thumb and fingers of your right hand. The back of this hand should be facing you. (see figure 2)

3. Hold the other corner marked (B) with your left hand. Fold the paper (towards corner A) over the back of your right hand fingers. (see figure 3)

4. Do this twice and a pointed tip should be formed. Adjust the bag so that you cannot see any daylight through the pointed end of the bag. (see figure 4)

5. Turn corner (B) into the inside of the bag. Make two small cuts in the folded in sections to form a flap. Turn the flap in to secure the bag. (see figure 5)

Handy Tip
For smaller bags, useful when pressure piping small areas, begin with a smaller triangle of greaseproof paper.

Figure 1

Figure 2

Figure 3

Figure 4

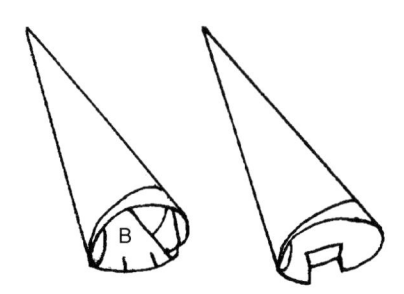

Figure 5

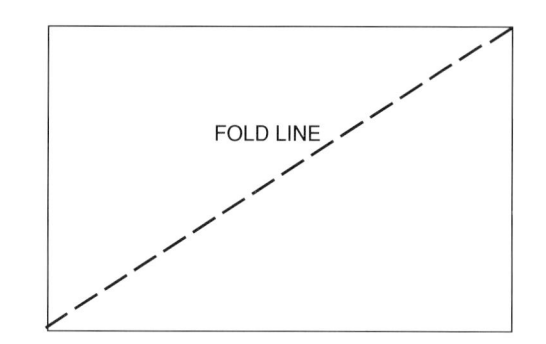

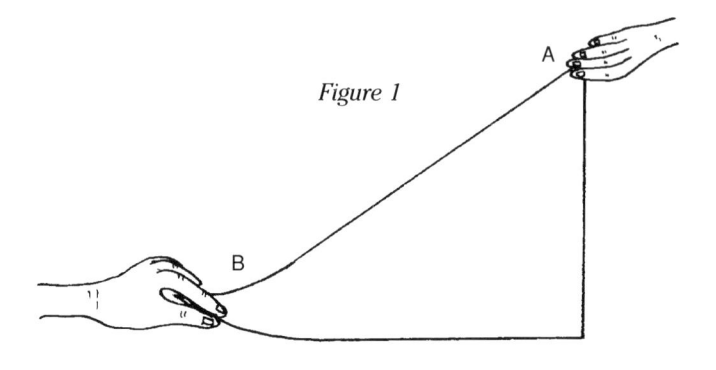

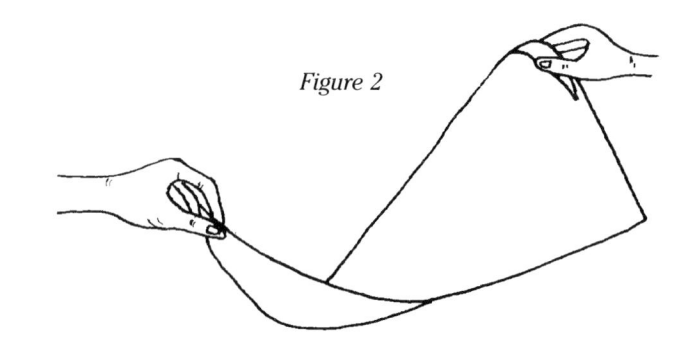

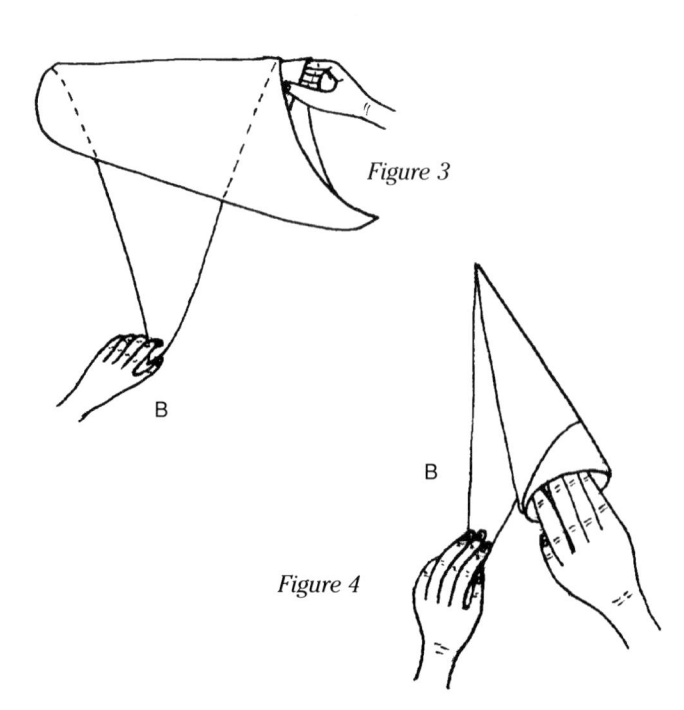

Filling the bag

Never over fill your bags. It is a terrible temptation I know but it just isn't worth it. A little icing will go a lot further than you think particularly if you are making pieces of filigree, lace or extension work. Normally the icing in the bag begins to change consistency well before you run out, making it necessary to change your bag anyway.

To fill the bag place a piping tube into it and hold the bag with the point facing downwards. Snip off sufficient bag to enable the end of the tube to show through.

Fill the bag by taking a small scoop of prepared royal icing on one side of a crank handled palette knife and inserting this deep into the bag. (see figure 6) Draw the top edges of the bag together over the knife which should be withdrawn at this stage. (see figure 7)

Fold in the sides and the top of the bag until there is no remaining gap between the bag and icing. (see figure 8)

The filled bag is now ready for use.

Using the bag

There are a number of basic piping techniques you will need when attempting the cake designs in this book all of which are explained here.

1. LINES using piping tubes Nos. 2,1,0,00.

Fill a piping bag with a no.1 tube and some royal icing. Hold the bag in one hand as you would a pencil and at an angle of about 40-45 deg. with the tip of the tube touching the work surface. Rest the little finger and wrist of your piping hand on the work surface as you begin to pipe, this will help to steady you.

Press on the creased top of the bag with the thumb and when the icing begins to emerge from the tube allow it to stick to the work surface.

Continue to press, lifting the bag about 25mm (1") and bringing it gently towards you. Keep your eye on the direction in which you want the line to follow.

When you have piped just short of the length of line required, stop pressing on the bag. The icing will immediately cease to run. Bring the piping tube down to the work surface, pulling the iced line very slightly as you do so.

This makes a neat, straight line.

ONLY USE ONE HAND TO HOLD YOUR PIPING BAG. Your other hand may steady your wrist as you begin but try not to rely on this. Both hands will have plenty to do when you pipe more complex pieces of work.

Figure 6

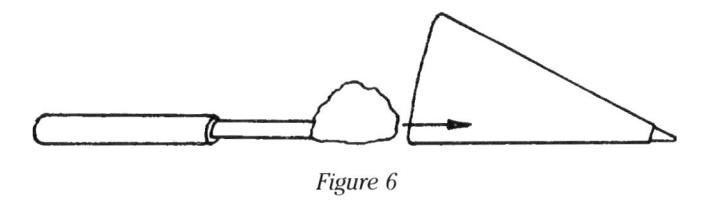

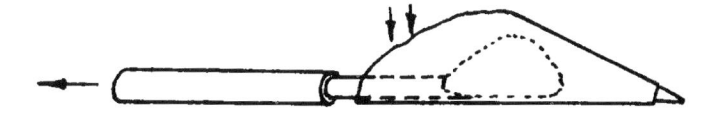

Figure 7

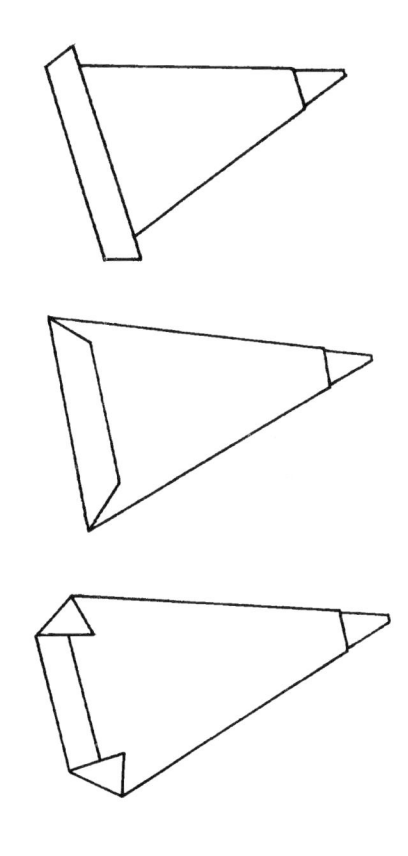

Figure 8

Curved lines - Cornelli

To pipe a curved line proceed as for the straight line until the icing is stuck to the work surface. Keep pressing gently on the bag and lift your wrist just clear, moving it in a continuous smooth curve. Always look at the direction you wish to go not the line of icing or where its been.

Cornelli consists of continuous wavy lines of icing with a "swiss roll" curve at the start and end. The iced lines should not touch each other at any point. It is important to learn this piping technique as it is quite easy to master and is often used to cover up errors, breaks and cracks in ornaments, etc.

Dots

These are frequently used to finish floating extension work in a softened form. Fill a piping bag with royal icing and a no. 1, 0, or 00 piping tube. Hold the bag at an angle of 90 deg. (vertically) to the work surface with the end of the tube just clear. Gently press the bag holding it steady until you have made the size of dot you want. Stop pressing and lift the bag quickly. This produces a dot with a tail.

For dots without tails use softened icing and, when you have made the size of dot you want, stop pressing on the bag. Lift the tube slowly.

Snail's Trail

This technique is most frequently used to finish the bottom edge of a cake either alone or with the addition of a narrow ribbon above.

If you intend to use it under extension work, it must always be applied before attempting any other side decoration.

Fill a piping bag with royal icing and a no. 1 or 2 tube. Hold the bag at an angle of approximately 40° to the work surface and pipe out a small dot pulling the tail towards you. Do not stop pressing on the bag. When the tail is about 3mm ($^1/_8$") long hold the bag over the end of the tail and pipe another sideways dot over the edge. Repeat this process to form a continuous line of sideways dots (plain shells) and lines all joined together. Repeat until you have completed the required distance. Do not break the line unless you have to. Any untidy ends can be neatened by softly brushing with a no. 1. paintbrush as you go.

Plate 4 - Example of piping techniques

Run-Out Techniques

A beautifully piped run-out often provides the finishing touch for a celebration cake. There are several varieties of run-out you can use on a cake these include outlined, pressure piped and built up pressure piped run-outs. I have described these three in this book as they have been used from time to time on some of the cakes featured.

Outlined run-outs

These, as their name implies, consist of an outline of royal icing filled with very soft royal icing which levels off to form a very flat surface. The whole can then be painted to produce the finished effect.

1. Trace around the Oast Houses on page 100 and transfer this to a piece of white card. Place under cellophane. Tape down the sides of the card and cellophane so that it will lie flat. (see figure 1)

2. Bring some royal icing to peaking consistency and gradually stir in lemon juice, drop by drop to make a very soft royal icing the consistency of single cream.

To test if you have achieved the correct consistency, trail some of the softened icing from your spoon onto the rest and count evenly to 10. The icing should level off between 8 and 9. If it takes less than 8 it is too soft. Add more peaking consistency icing and stir until it becomes level between 8 and 9. If it takes longer than 9 to level add more lemon juice, drop by drop until it levels out between 8 and 9.

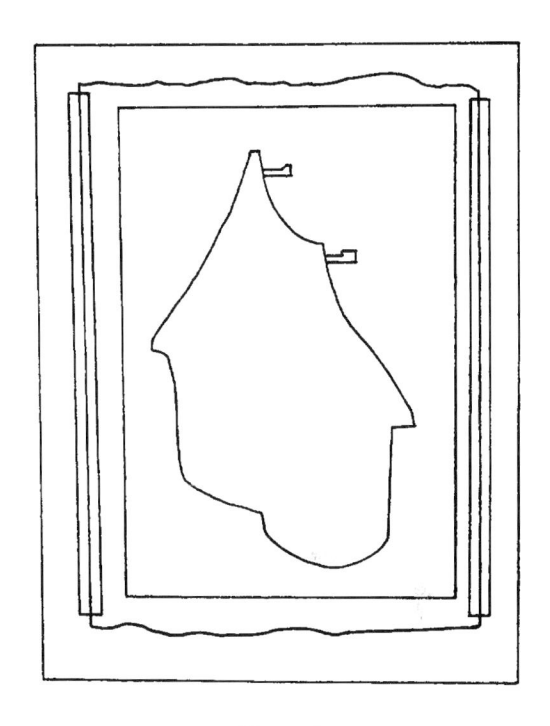

Figure 1

> ### Handy Tip
> Lemon juice helps to produce a stronger run-out when it has set.

3. Leave the prepared run-out icing for a couple of minutes as this allows some of the bubbles to rise to the surface. Break these as they appear.

4. Turn the icing onto a flat surface and paddle it. To do this draw a palette knife backwards and forwards quickly through it with the flat of the blade on top. This will help to remove any bubbles in the icing.

5. Scoop the paddled icing into a piping bag and cut off enough of the bag to represent a no 2 tube. Force the icing through this bag into another bag. Do not cut the end off the second bag.

Fill several bags in this way.

6. Fill a piping bag with some softened royal icing and a no 1 tube and place the tip of the tube under a damp cloth.

7. Use this icing to outline the traced shape, taking care that there are no gaps in your piped lines. Neaten your work by smoothing the edges with a paintbrush. (see figure 2)

8. Fill the outlined shape by gradually running the softened icing into it. Begin at the finest point and work, from side to side, ensuring that all the wet areas of icing are continually moved until the whole area is filled. (see figure 3) Prick any air bubbles as they appear, these can help to weaken the run-out and can make it more fragile to remove. Once the area is filled it should have a domed appearance. As the icing shrinks slightly when drying it levels off and if the run-out is insufficiently filled dents and puckers may occur. (see figure 4)

9. For best results, the run-out should be placed approximately 225mm (9") under an angle poised lamp to dry. This will ensure a smooth shine.

10. The run-out should be ready to paint after twelve hours and ready to remove from the cellophane after two days.

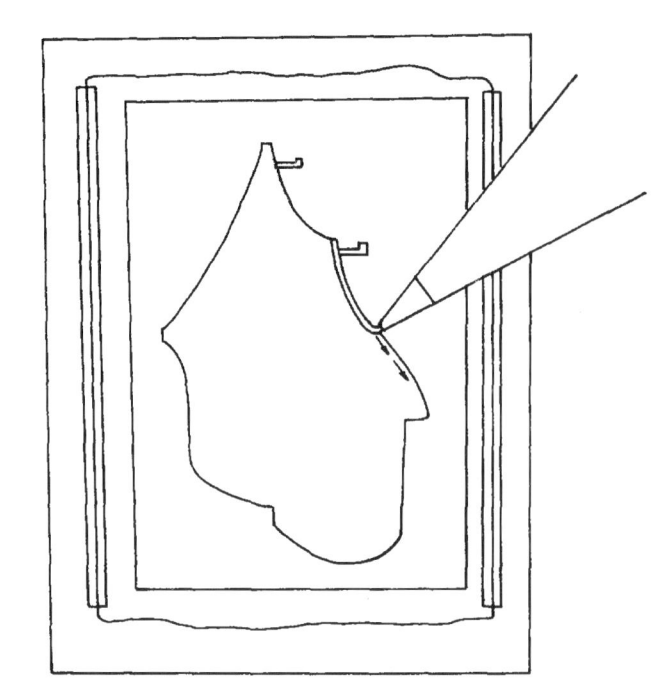

Figure 2

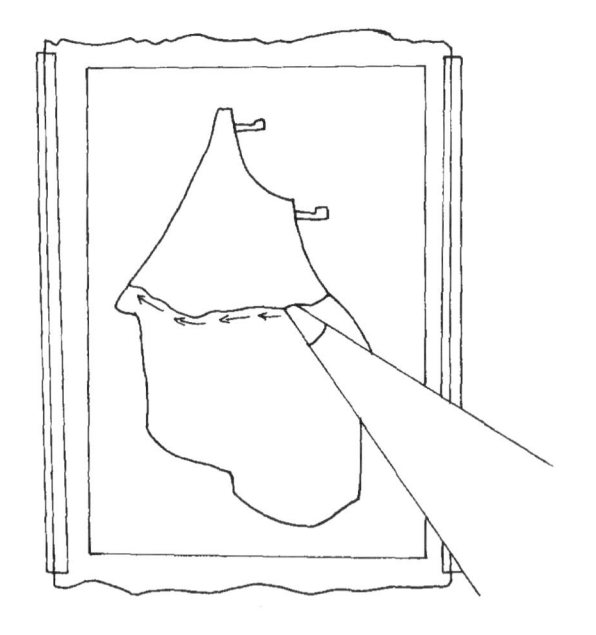

Figure 3

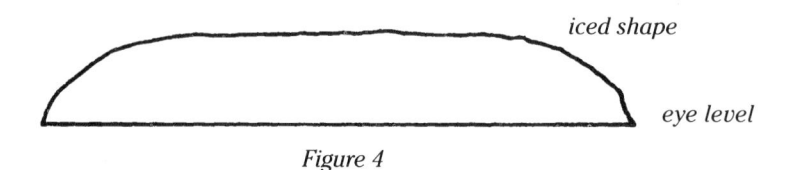

iced shape

eye level

Figure 4

Pressure piped run-outs

This technique can be used to produce a great deal of detail in your piece of work. Fingers and toes, chubby cheeks, frills, etc., are all possible once you have mastered the basics. It is also possible to create a feeling of depth to the piece if you remember to work from the background towards the foreground.

Best of Friends featured on page 35 was piped using this technique.

1. Trace the pattern below and number the areas as shown. With pressure piping you need to work from the background towards the foreground. By numbering the areas that appear to be furthest away from you and gradually working towards the front you will find it is easier to remember where you are when piping them in. (see figure 1)

2. Cover the traced pattern with some cellophane and tape down the corners. Make sure the cellophane is as flat as possible.

3. Place some royal icing into a cup and bring to peaking consistency. Gradually add water, drop by drop, stirring after each addition until the icing resembles thick double cream.

4. To test if the icing is of the correct consistency lift the knife over its surface to create a trail and start counting. After counting to four, gently agitate the knife up and down until the icing levels out. It should become level by the count of eight.

If the icing levels before seven it is too soft and needs to have more peaking consistency icing added to it. If it levels out after nine it is too stiff and needs another drop or two of water.

5. Once you are happy, place a little of the icing into a piping bag and snip off the end to represent a size 1 piping tube. Pipe a little icing onto the work surface and, keeping the end of the bag in the icing, agitate it slightly. If it forms a smooth rounded shape and only spreads out slightly, it is ready for use. This run-down icing is known as pressure piped icing.

6. Fill several bags with the icing and keep the tips under a damp cloth. Cut off the tip of each bag as you come to use it.

Handy Tip

You can afford to add the water a few drops at a time when you begin. Do not become impatient and add too much at a time once the icing begins to soften as it will change consistency very quickly once it starts to turn.

Figure 1

7. Fill each set of numbered sections e.g. 1, then 2, etc. (see figure 2) Leave each to dry for about 20 minutes before filling adjacent areas. For hair use a paintbrush to stroke the icing until it begins to dry and streak. Leave it to set. You may wish to pipe over the hair a couple of times to make it thicker. This is perfectly acceptable just make sure the section underneath is quite dry before attempting to over pipe it.

8. To make chubby cheeks, pipe out the face and leave until you can just see a slight skin forming over the surface. Replace your piping bag under the icing at the point you wish the raised cheek to appear. Slowly pipe a little icing from the bag, keeping the tip of the bag in place. Stop pressing when you have achieved the finish you want. Gently remove the bag and if necessary neaten the surface of the piped area with a paintbrush.

9. Leave the run-out 225mm (9") under an angle poised lamp as each section is completed and when finished leave for approximately two hours before painting.

10. Once dry, paint in details, eyes, mouth, etc. After at least twenty four hours, remove the run-out from the cellophane. To remove run your fingers either side of the run-out to create a ridge, this will help to loosen it. Draw the run-out to the side of your work surface. Pull down each side gently, keeping your other hand under the cellophane. Then pull one side down and towards you allowing the run-out to slide off onto your hand. (see figure 3)

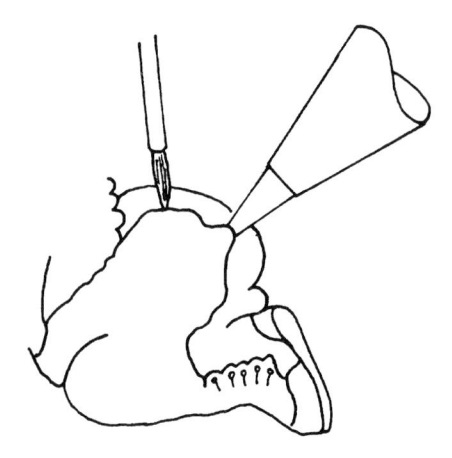

Figure 2

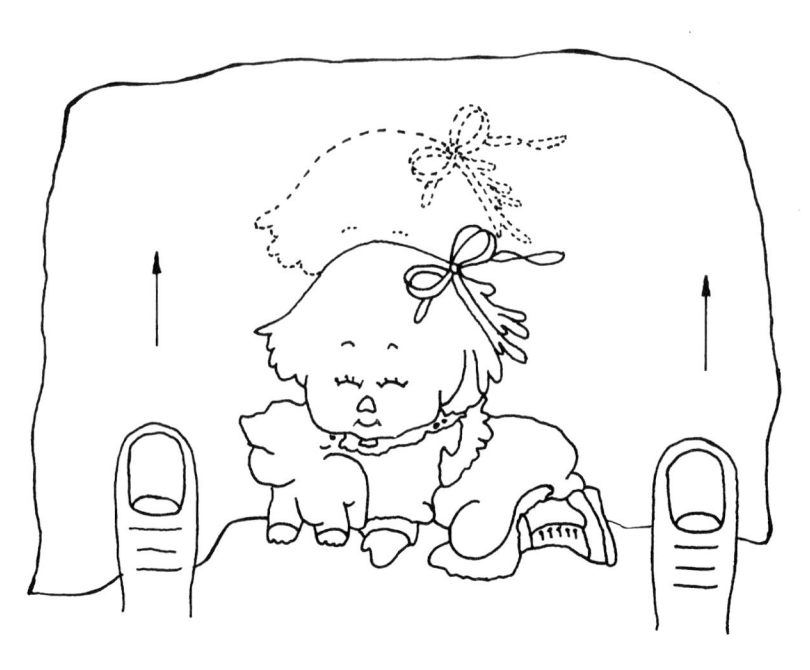

Figure 3

Best Of Friends

True Love

Took third place - Open Masterclass at the London Christmas Exhibition 1990

Pressure piped built up run-out

Worked directly onto the cake's surface these run-outs give the appearance of three dimensions. The castle featured on the Fairytale Castle cake was made using this technique.

1. Trace the pattern on page 92 and inscribe it onto the cake.

2. Make up some pressure piped icing and fill several bags with this. Mark the bags 'P'.

3. Place about two tablespoons of pressure piped icing in a cup and add water drop by drop stirring constantly until the icing resembles whipping cream.

To test if the consistency is correct draw a knife over the icing and count until the icing levels itself without help. This should take between a count of 6 - 7.

4. Fill some piping bags with this run-out icing and cut off the tip of the bag to represent a no. 1 piping tube. Mark the bags 'R'.

5. Using a paintbrush in one hand and the run-out icing 'P' pipe a thin layer of icing over the entire castle area of the pattern. Use the paintbrush to draw the icing to the corners of the design. (see figure 1)

6. Leave to dry completely. This will take approximately 4 hours.

7. Overpipe the sections (see figure 2) using the pressure piped icing 'P' and drawing the icing down to the edge.

8. Overpipe the sections (see figure 3) using the pressure piped icing and drawing the icing over the under layers with a paintbrush to hide the edges. (see figure 3)

9. Overpipe the sections (see figure 4) finishing each section as in step 8.

10. Pipe in the battlements, drawing a paintbrush through the run-out icing to create definition. Pipe in the windows and flags to finish. (see figure 5)

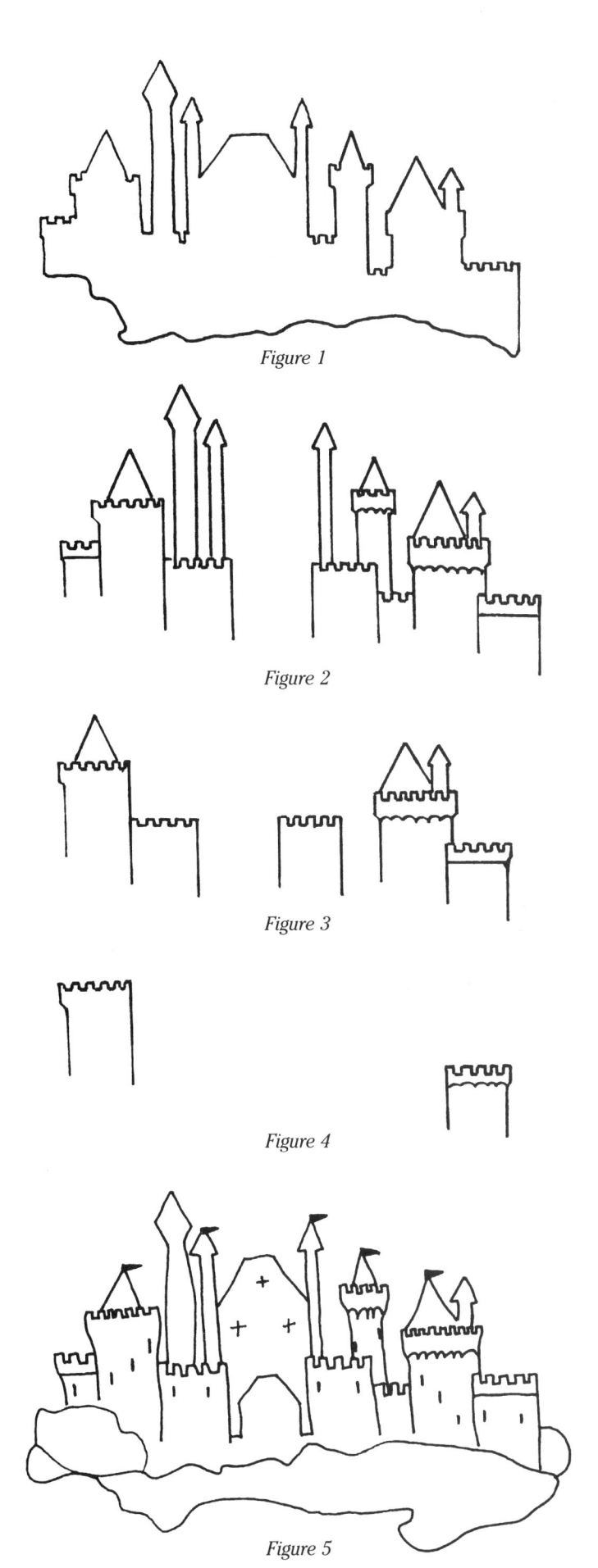

Figure 1

Figure 2

Figure 3

Figure 4

Figure 5

Brush Embroidery

Brush embroidery can be a delight to the eye. It is very dainty and looks particularly elegant when executed in white on cream as can be seen in Cream Sensation featured on pages 82 and 83. Subjects for brush embroidery are often taken from nature, for example flowers, butterflies etc.

The technique consists of piping a mixture of royal icing and piping jelly around the outside edge of the subject. Some of this mixture is then gradually drawn downwards and towards the centre to create a shaded effect.

To create the brush embroidery featured on Cream Sensation following the directions given.

1. Trace the pattern for Cream Sensation on page 94 making sure it is suitable for the size of cake you are working on.

2. Place the tracing onto the cake taking care to keep the traced side away from the cake's surface. Prick a few guidelines onto the sugarpaste with a pin. Try to use as few guidelines as possible. (see figure 1)

3. Following your pattern which must be next to your work gradually fill in the remaining pattern lines, gently scoring them in with a pin.

4. Place about two tablespoons of royal icing into a cup and bring to peaking consistency. Add a scant $1/4$ teaspoon of piping gel. Mix together.

5. Take a piping bag fitted with a No 1 tube and fill with some of the mixture. Working from the background to the foreground pipe a single line of icing over the outer edge of the furthest petal.

6. Pipe another line just inside and touching the outer. Make this line thinner as you approach the lower edge of the petal. (see figure 2)

Figure 1

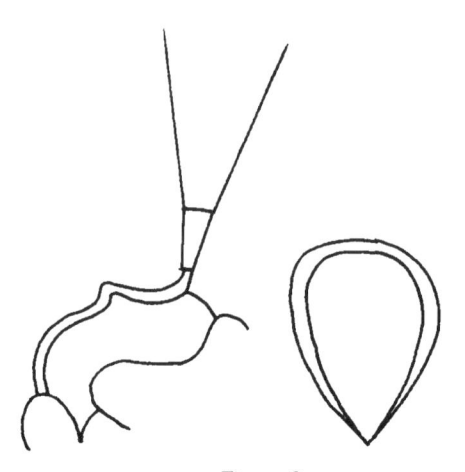

Figure 2

7. Using a damp No. 1 paintbrush at an angle of approximately 45° draw the icing down and towards the base of the petal in the direction of the arrows. A fine coating of icing should cover the centre and appear to be almost transparent by the time you reach the base. (see figure 3)

Handy tip

An egg cup filled with a little water and a damp paper towel are useful items of equipment. You can then dip the paintbrush into the water and quickly draw it across the towel. This ensures the paintbrush is not too damp or too dry.

Figure 3

8. If you are working on a large rose petal work on one half at a time always draw the icing down and towards the centre ensuring that you do not have a centre line. (see figure 4)

9. Continue in this way until all the pattern has been filled. Any petals which lie adjacent to each other should be worked to give the effect of tucking under. Only leave a clear edge on one side while the other can be allowed to lie flat. The centre of the petal should be coated with a very thin, almost transparent layer of icing.

Colour can be incorporated if desired. Always begin with the palest shade working in towards the centre. Then overpipe the edge with a darker shade and draw this toward the centre as described to create the effect of shading.

Any stamens should be piped in at the end to complete the decoration.

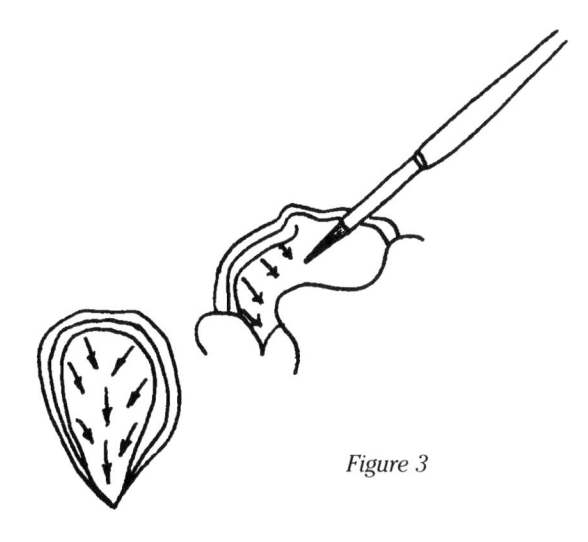

Figure 4

Extension Work

Extension work is one of the most versatile of all cake decorating techniques. It may be piped in a variety of colours and shapes from purest white on white to a rainbow cascade. Fine curtains of royal iced strands teamed with lace and embroidery will produce the daintiest of cakes. Made to float and combined with art work or flowers, it imparts an air of sophistication to the finished piece.

Always use the finest piping tubes you can cope with, numbers 0 or 00 will produce the best results. The finer the tube you use the more delicate your work will be. Floating extension work should be very fine with no hint as to how it was created.

Above all do not be afraid to experiment. Just because you have never used a number 0 or 00 piping tube before does not mean you will not be able to do so. Many of my students have been surprised at how easy it is to work with fine tubes once they have taken the plunge. Remember my golden rule if you can do something once you have proved you can do it again. There is no such word as can't only don't panic. It takes time to build your confidence so do not try to rush things.

Everyone needs to work at their own pace to achieve success and sufficient practice is most important.

A few basic rules

1. Always complete the decoration on the cake board and cake's base before you begin the sides.

2. Work in a good light with the light source on the side from which you are working. An angle poised lamp or next to a window in good daylight is ideal for this.

3. There is no secret to producing beautiful extension work. Practise and the use of the finest tubes for your dropped strings and lace off pieces will help. Piping tubes 0 and 00 are ideal for this.

4. If using a fixed bridge, pipe this with a no. 1 piping tube. If using a floating bridge pipe this with a no. 0 piping tube. Always work with an even piping pressure throughout.

5. Never try to cut corners or become worried if you cannot achieve the result you expect the first time. Fine extension work can take some time to master but is well worth the effort.

6. If you find you can achieve something once e.g. piping a few dropped strings, attaching a piece of lace, etc. you will be able to do so again.

7. Deal with breakages as they occur, it makes life much easier.

8. Always work at eye level and make sure you are comfortable before you begin any piping.

9. Sieved royal icing should be used with very fine tubes e.g. 0 or 00. To sieve, take some royal icing at peaking consistency and add enough water to make soft peaks which will just tip over slowly. If using colour add this before any water. Place the icing onto a piece of butter muslin and draw up the sides. Holding the bag firmly, flick your wrist downwards to help the icing move towards the centre of the muslin. Place the bag into the palm of your free hand with the bulk of the bag resting between your thumb and first finger.

Twist the bag whilst applying pressure to it with your thumb and first finger. The icing should pass through quite easily. Let this fall into a clean bowl. Only remove the wet icing left on your hands. Do not allow any dry pieces of icing to fall into the bowl. This is most important as it will destroy all your messy, hard work. Cover the icing with a damp cloth.

Fixed extension work

This type of extension work combines the beauty of delicate dropped strings with the strength of a permanent bridge. To prepare the cake, first mark out your cake's side pattern as described in the pattern making section. Always make sure you have completed any decoration you wish to place under the extension work, for example snail's trail etc. before attempting the extension work itself.

Handy tip

If this is your first attempt at extension work use a straight line for the top edge and keep the length of the dropped strings to 25mm (1") deep. This will make it easier for you to work and help you to gain confidence. (see figure 1) Once you are happy and able to pipe extension work with a certain amount of ease, progress onto the more advanced patterns and practise piping deeper dropped strings.

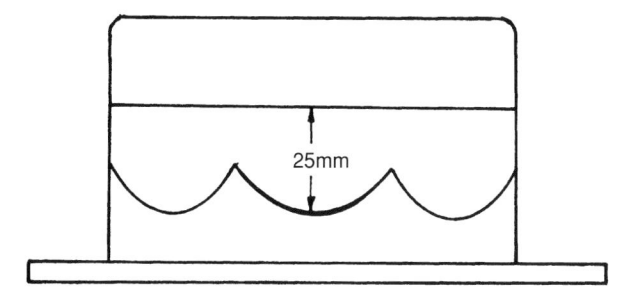

Figure 1

To pipe the bridge

1. Fill a piping bag with some royal icing and a no.1 tube. Touch the piping tube against one of the points on the lower inscribed bridge line. Ensure your piped line is attached.

2. Keeping a constant pressure on the bag, gently bring the piped line away from the cake side. This line will begin to curve.

Continue to pipe the curve until it is just short of the desired length. (see figure 2a and 2b)

3. Release the pressure on the piping bag. Touch the line against the next point on your inscribed pattern. The piped curved line will flop back against the cake side.

4. Repeat the next curve in the same way taking care to pipe the same depth of curve.

5. Once you have mastered this technique, pipe the scalloped curves in as continuous a line as possible around the cake side.

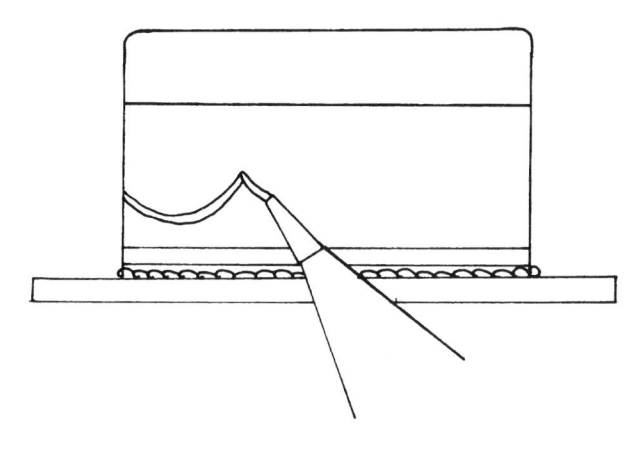

Figure 2a

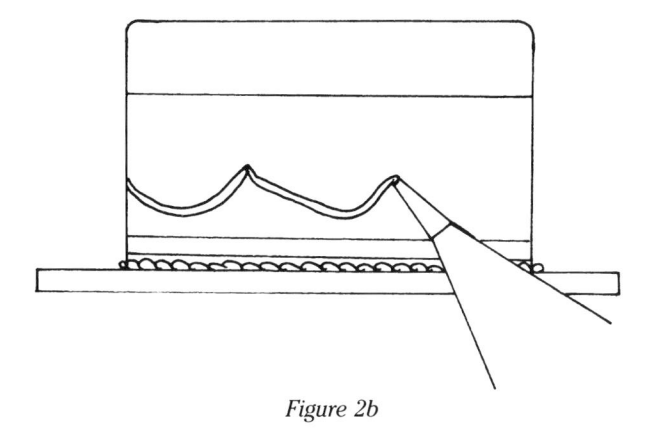

Figure 2b

6. If you break this line, gently smooth any joins with a damp paintbrush to achieve a neat finish.

7. Hold the cake at an angle and look down at the bridge line. Check that there are no gaps between the piped line and the cake side. If there are, gently use a paintbrush to touch the piped line against the cake. If the line has dried and will not move, fill in the gaps by piping in a little softened icing and neaten off with a paintbrush.

8. Leave to dry for 15 minutes then pipe a second line over the first, ensuring that it is as even as possible.

9. Repeat until you have between 8 and 10 bridge lines attached to the cake. (see figure 3)

10. Try to ensure there is no daylight to be seen between any of the bridge lines.

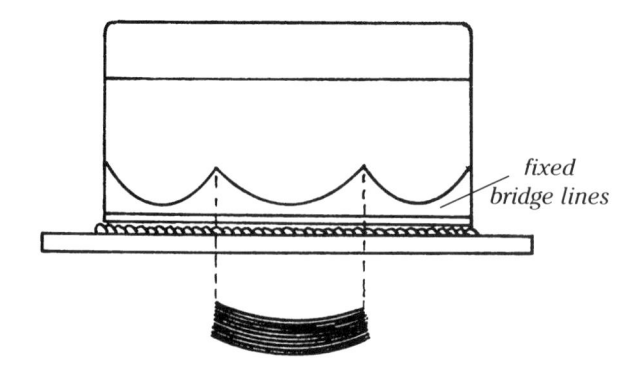

Handy tip

As a final test to see if the bridge is firm, lift the cake on its board about 12mm ($^1/_2$") and allow it to drop.
If the bridge remains firm and no areas of daylight appear it is safe to continue.

You should be able to hold the cake with the bridge at eye level and only see one curved line. If you can see more than one line, (see figure 4a, 4b) remove that section and repeat, slightly overlapping the ends and making it neat with a paintbrush.

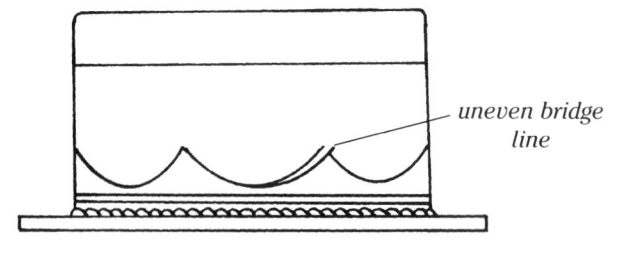

Figure 3 — fixed bridge lines

Figure 4a — uneven bridge line

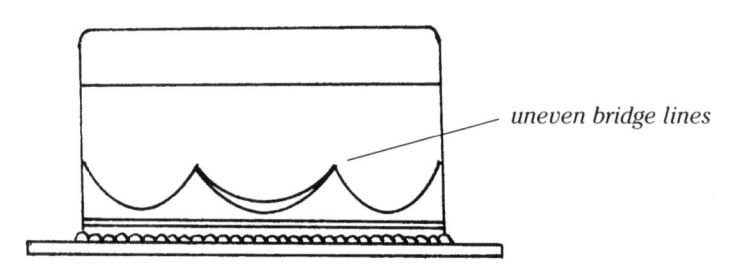

Figure 4b — uneven bridge lines

Piping the dropped strings

1. Place the cake at eye level with a good light source on the same side as you intend to work.

2. Fill a piping bag fitted with a no. 0 or 00 piping tube and some sieved royal icing.

3. Touch the tip of the piping tube against the top edge of your pattern. Press out enough icing to form a firm attachment.

4. In one continuous movement, gently bring the piping bag away from the cake at an angle of approximately 45°. Apply a continuous even pressure to the bag and pipe a strand of icing away from the cake's side. (see figure 1)

5. Stop applying pressure just short of the bridge and pull the strand down slightly until it is straight. Touch this to the bridge. This strand is known as a dropped string. (see figure 2)

6. Neaten the base of the dropped string by tucking it under the bridge with the damp paintbrush.

7. Repeat the above until the desired sections of dropped strings have been piped.

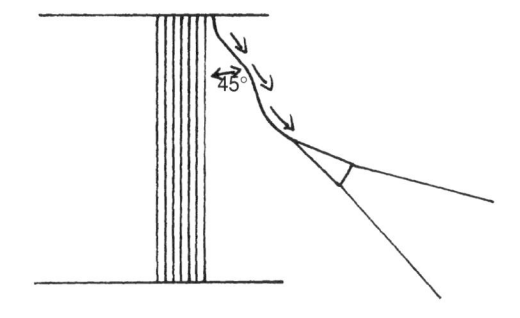

Figure 1

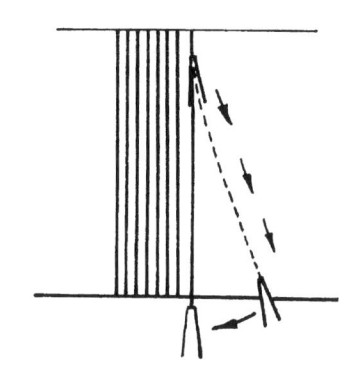

Figure 2

Notes on piping dropped strings

1) The strings should all be straight and even. If you can pipe another in the gap between any two, the strings are too far apart.

2) As you look through the side of the extension work only one continuous line should be visible. (see figure 1)

Do not worry if you cannot achieve this at first it can take many months to perfect the technique.

Figure 1

Handy tip

When piping check every inch to make sure you are not sloping the strings. If you are and the situation is not too bad, pipe another line as closely to the previous work as possible. Ensure the base is straight and use this as a "plumb line".

If your work is very crooked it is better to remove the crooked section then continue as above.
(see figures 2a & b)

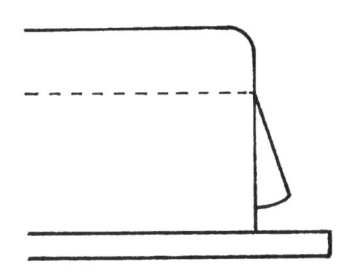

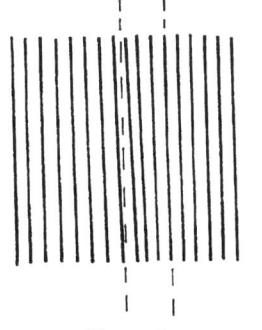

Figure 2a    *Figure 2b*

3) To ensure the lines are evenly spaced place the tube as close to the top of the previous line as possible without actually touching it. Watch the line as it is piped and when you are ready to stop piping check the bottom and top are the same distance apart. Attach the line to the bridge.

4) If you break one or more strings, do not worry, it is very easy to repair broken strings. Using a pin, remove any top or bottom pieces that have remained intact. Gently pipe a new string in place, ensuring that the piping tube does not itself come into contact with any other strings. Pipe a second string if necessary once the first is dry.

5) When piping onto a curved bridge always remember the distance you are piping flat against the cake, is less than the distance to the bridge.

You will need to allow for this when you begin piping. Pipe the top edge closely opening out the distance of the loops as you come down onto the bridge. As you approach the central portion of the curve the distance between the bottom edges of the strings will become noticeably wider. Do not worry about this, it is perfectly acceptable as can be seen on Christmas Time featured on page 18.

Finishing extension work

There are several different decorative styles you can use to finish your extension work. Dots, a line around the bottom bridge, loops of equal and different depths are all useful and relatively easy to work. A few examples of different finishing touches are shown here for future reference, however it is much more fun to use a finish which is all your own.

Extension work can be made to look more special if finished with fine lace off pieces or poor man's lace, see the section on Embroidery and Lace.

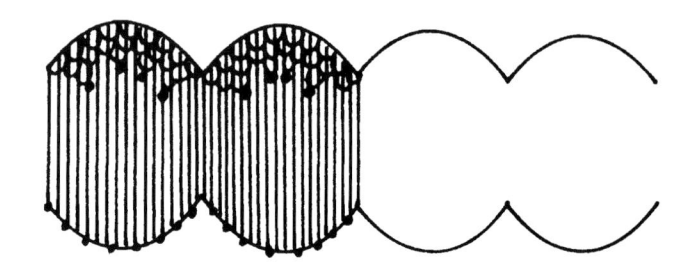

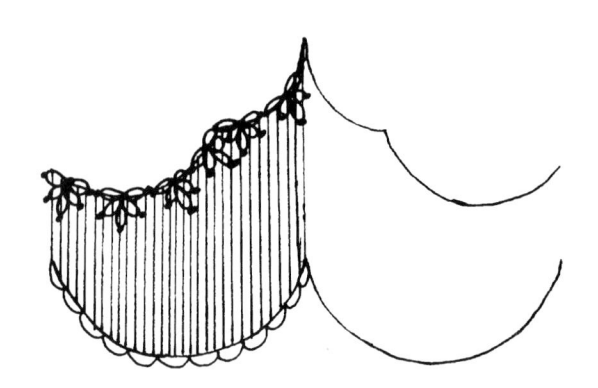

Castle in the Air
Took second place - Masterclass Sugarpaste at the Southdown Exhibition 1990

Floating Extension Work

Before piping floating extension work you need to prepare two patterns. One for the side and the other for your floating bridge. When piped, this floating bridge provides a temporary support to which the dropped strings are attached. This will then be removed to leave the dropped strings apparently floating on air.

When making the pattern for the floating bridge try to be as accurate with your measurements as possible. To test whether the pattern is the correct size always follow the directions given. Never assume you are right. If you are wrong and have corrected your error you will find it much easier to join the sections together. If they overlap slightly juggle them apart, remembering to line up any curves on the cake side with the curves on your floating bridge. If you need to adjust the length of a section because it is too short, add a small line of icing to join the section to its neighbour. If on the other hand it is too long, use a paintbrush to dampen the end and allow this softened area to fall away. Then join the shortened end to its neighbour. If you find that you break the floating bridge overpipe the line using a no. 0 tube. Do not be tempted to use a no. 1 tube. The thicker the iced line the more difficult it will be to remove after the extension work has been piped.

Once you begin to pipe the dropped strings you must be careful to ensure only the icing or a lightly dampened paintbrush come into contact with the floating bridge. This is most important. Do not attempt to remove the bridge until the extension work has been completed. If you intend to decorate the dropped strings do this before the bridge is removed as any breakages are more easily repaired if the original bridge is still in position. The dots or lines which are a featured around the bottom of floating extension work add strength, by joining the strings together in pairs or forming a continuous line linking all the dropped strings together. They also add interest and neaten the ends of the strings in a decorative fashion.

If you are a novice try piping floating extension work in small sections.

Floating extension work in sections

This is particularly suitable for novices as working in small sections helps to increase confidence and the odd break will not cause too many problems.

1. Mark the cake into an even number of curves exactly following the section for fixed bridge pattern making.

2. Make the pattern for the floating bridge.

(a) Measure the diameter of the cake and divide by two. Using a pair of compasses opened to this size draw a circle onto a sheet of paper. Mark this circle c/l.

(b) Draw another circle over the c/l 25mm(1") larger. Mark this circle F. Using a protractor divide the circle into 8,16 etc. (see figure 1) The number of divisions should equal the number of curves inscribed on the cake's side.

Figure 1

(c) Using one segment, find the centre by drawing a straight line connecting points A and B. Measure this line and divide in half.

Mark this point C. Draw a line from point D passing through point C. and touching line F. mark this G.

(d) Inscribe a curve between points A and B, the centre of which should just touch point G. (see figure 2)

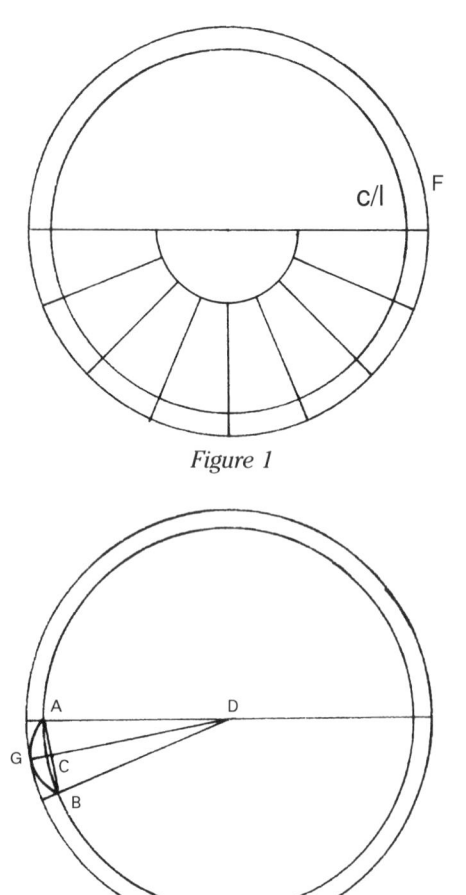

Figure 2

3. Tape a straight piece of paper to the finished pattern and place under cellophane. The paper tag will allow you to move the pattern under the cellophane.

4. Fill a piping bag with some royal icing and using a no. 1 piping tube. Pipe a line of royal icing around the curve.

5. Remove the curve from the cellophane and hold it against the cake's side. Line up the points on the curved bridge with those inscribed onto the cake's side. You should be able to pipe a dropped string close to the edge of the bridge without the centre of the string touching the cake. (see figure 3) If this is not possible, cut the pattern curve a little deeper and try again.

6. Fill a piping bag with some royal icing and a no. 0 piping tube. Pipe a line of royal icing around the curve. Overpipe this line. Move the pattern and pipe sufficient curves to complete the bridge. Leave to dry for 15 minutes.

7. Assemble two brackets close together in front of the centre of one inscribed curve on the cake.

8. Gently ease the curve off the cellophane by running your fingers along one side and inserting a crank handled palette knife under it.

9. Place on to the bridge joining it to the cake with a small dot of royal icing at each end.(see figure 4) Pipe your dropped strings and leave to dry for 30 mins. Remove the brackets by pressing on them and pulling them free. (see figure 5)

10. Following the instructions for removing the continuous bridge, pipe a row of dots joining the dropped strings. Remove the bridge by dampening it with a little water on a paintbrush. Work on one half of each section at a time.

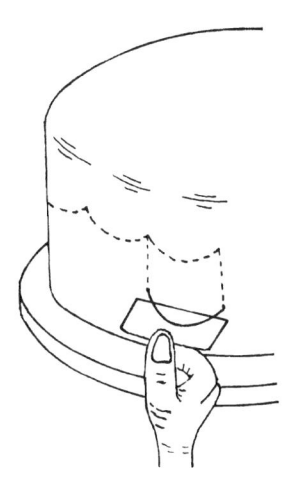

Figure 3

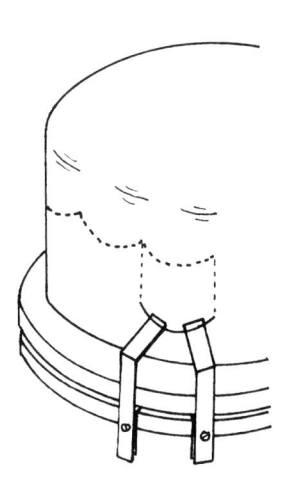

Figure 4

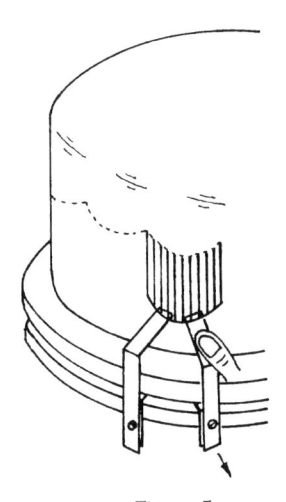

Figure 5

Handy tip

If you have covered your cake board with sugarpaste, place small pieces of paper on top to catch the damp icing as it falls from the bridge.

To pipe a continuous line of floating extension work

1. Prepare the pattern for the top edge of the floating extension work. Mark this onto your cake.

To construct the floating bridge

1. Make your pattern for the floating bridge.

2. Using a no.0 piping tube pipe round the curved edge of the pattern in four quarters. Overpipe each making sure there are no gaps and leave to dry for 15 minutes.

Remove the section by loosening the ends with your fingers see section on removing lace off-pieces . Ease the palette knife under one end of the line and run this smoothly along its length to free it completely. Repeat this procedure with the other sections. The sections of the circle are now ready for assembly and are known as the floating bridge lines.

3. Place the cake onto a second cake board the same size as that on which it has been attached. Do not stick this down.

4. Position the cake at eye level. Place the brackets between the two cake boards about 62mm (2^1/$_2$") apart. The top bar should be just above the snail's trail. The weight of the cake will hold the brackets in place.

5. Cut a piece of card roughly the same shape as one section of the floating bridge line. With great care lift the floating bridge in sections onto the shaped card using a paintbrush to move it. Place the sections onto the brackets. (see plate 1) Adjust their position until a complete circle is formed, the joins resting between the brackets. The curves should be equidistant from the cake sides. Join the sections with a little softened royal icing to form one continuous line. This is known as the floating bridge. (see plate 2) Pipe small dots of royal icing onto the brackets inside the floating bridge. These act as stops, thus ensuring the bridge cannot move out of position.

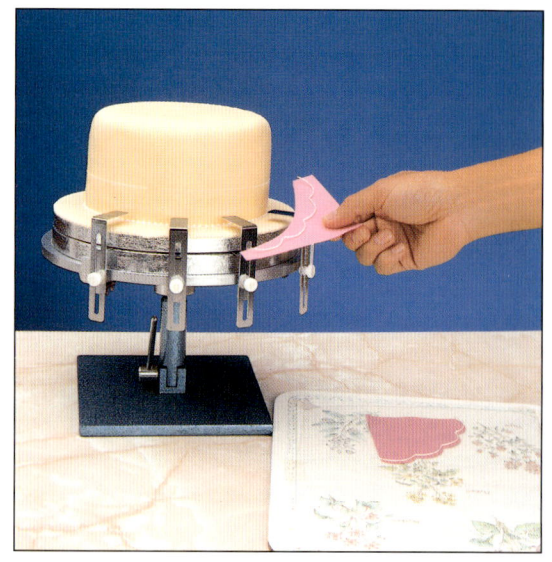

Plate 1

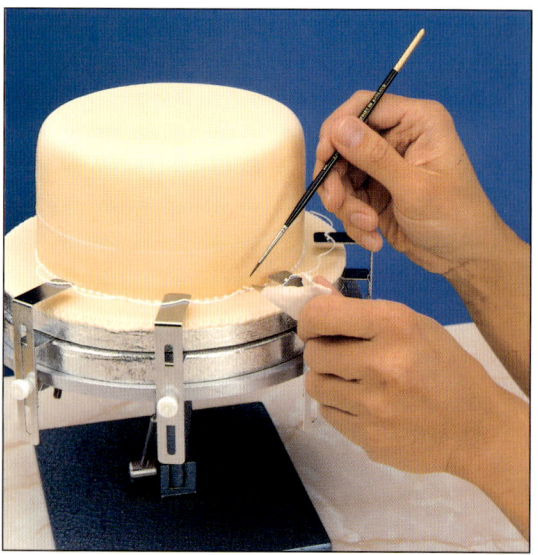

Plate 2

6. Using a 0 or 00 piping tube pipe a few dropped strings every 75 - 100mm (3-4") around the cake. Use the floating bridge as you would a fixed bridge taking care not to touch it with your tube. Tuck the base of each dropped string under the bridge with a damp paintbrush. Work very gently when touching this bridge as it is very delicate. These first few strings act as anchors to the bridge and help to keep it in place. (see plate 3) Leave to dry for 15 minutes. Very gently remove every other bracket by pressing down on the top and carefully pulling away. The bridge should remain in place. If the bridge appears to move LEAVE THAT BRACKET ALONE and move on to the next.

7. Pipe a continuous line of extension work around the cake. (see plate 4) Each group of anchor strings will need to be removed before the perfect strings can be piped into place. Dampen these strings with a paintbrush before removing them. Any remaining brackets within 50mm (2") of completed extension work sections can be removed at any time. This allows you more room to manoeuvre without risking damage.

Removing the floating bridge

Before you begin to remove the bridge fill two piping bags with icing. Fit one with a no. 0 piping tube, the other with the same sized tube as was used to pipe the dropped strings. Label these bags with the tube size and keep the tips of the tubes under a damp cloth. They will be needed to repair any damage which may occur.

1. Using a no. 0 piping tube and soft royal icing which will not hold a peak, pipe small dots linking every other dropped string above the floating bridge. These add strength to the finished piece and make removing the bridge easier. Always leave at least 3mm ($1/8$") above the bridge clear. (see figure 1)

2. Press down on the top of any remaining brackets. Gently slide the brackets from under the floating bridge.

At this point you will need extra patience and time. Do not try to rush the next few steps, if you do the hours of work you have put in so far could all be wasted. Don't worry if you follow the steps carefully and repair any damage as it occurs you should not have any difficulty in removing the bridge.

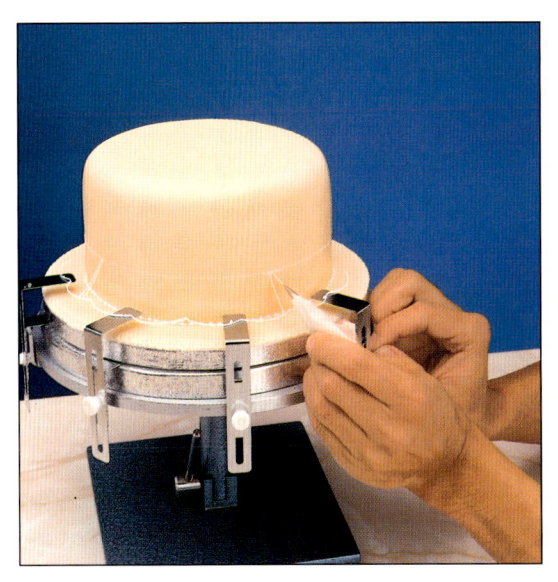

Plate 3

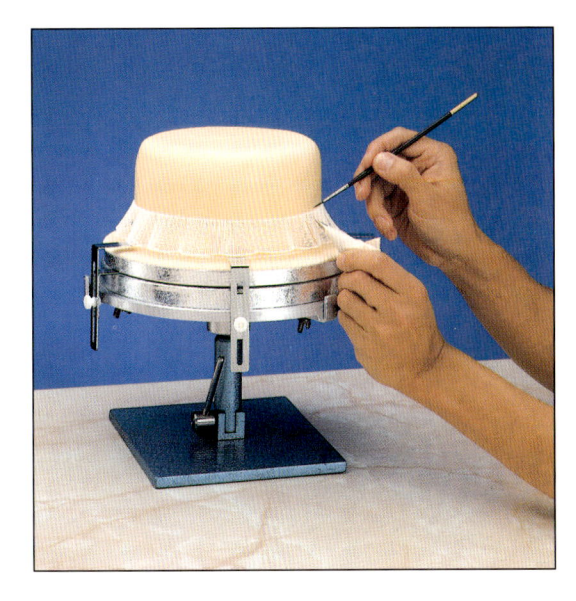

Plate 4

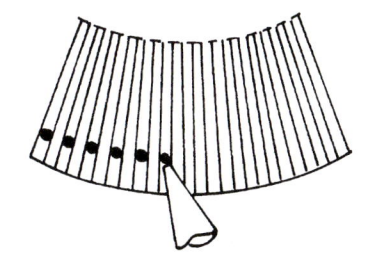

Figure 1

3. Using a no 0 or 1 paintbrush and a little water, gently dampen about 25mm (1") of the bridge. Do not use too much water as this will cause the floating bridge to collapse too quickly and the ends of the dropped strings will shrivel back too far. (see plate 5)

Handy tip

Place a small piece of paper on top of the cake board under the floating bridge. This will protect any decoration you may have on the board from becoming wet when the bridge section melts away.

---

4. To remove the section of bridge, gently roll the heavily dampened paintbrush along the front. The bridge should come away quite easily. If not, wet it a little more, then gently push down on the section with the paintbrush to free it.

Handy tip

Examine the bridge as you dampen it, the piped line should begin to look translucent and damp. If any of the dropped strings begin to look wet and shrivel they will probably need to be repaired before you add the finishing touches. See the section on trouble shooting.

---

5. Pipe in the final row of dots, connecting the dropped strings in pairs. (see plate 6 and figure 2)

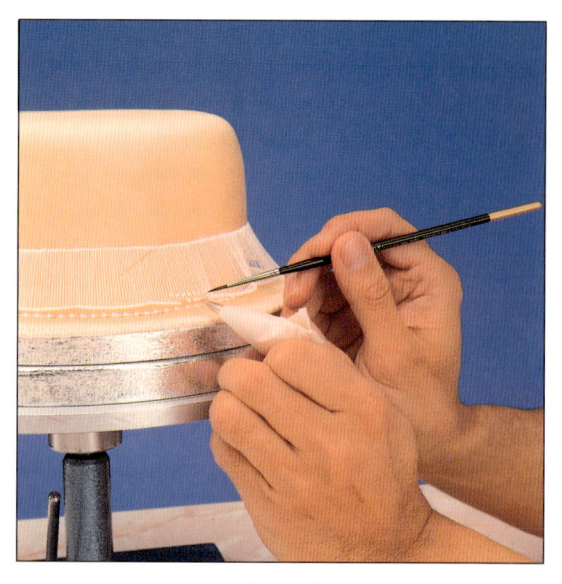

Plate 5

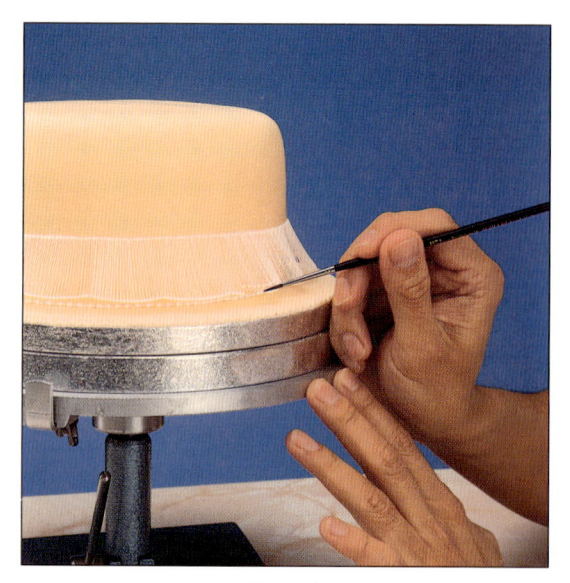

Plate 6

Figure 2

Lullaby

Golden Showers

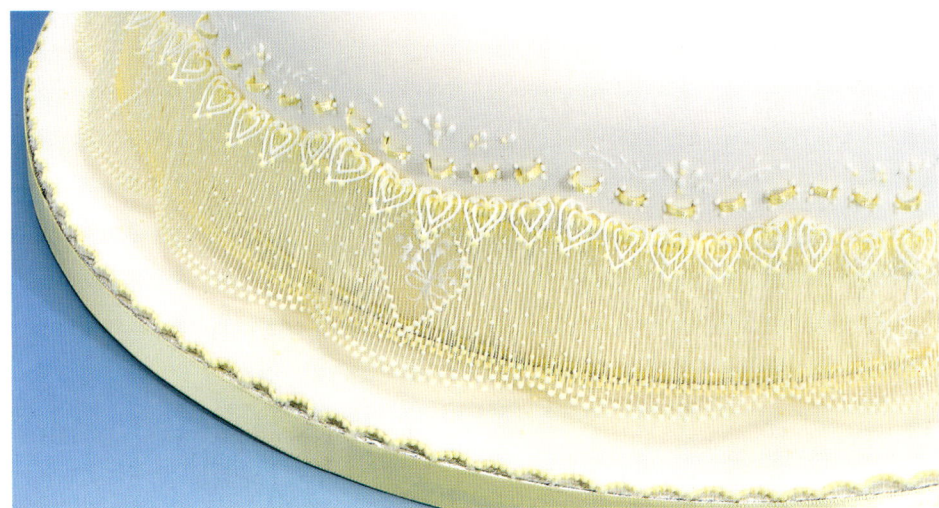

Golden Showers

Merry Christmas

To graduate the dropped strings

1. Pipe dots around the curve, etc. on the completed dropped string section, following the shape you wish to create. (see figure 3a, 3b)

2. Soften each individual dropped string at least 3mm (1/8") below these dots. Join the ends with dots to complete the required design. (see figure 4a, 4b)

Handy tip

Work on short sections at a time approximately 50mm (2") in length. The dots used in any design may be worked in colour if wished.

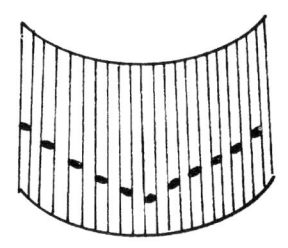

Figure 3a

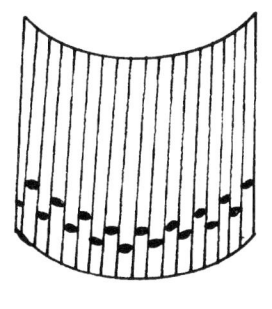

Figure 3b

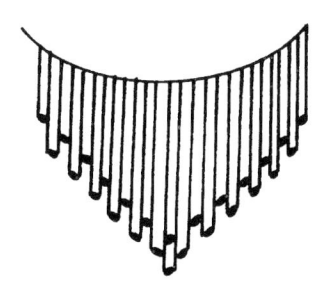

Figure 4a

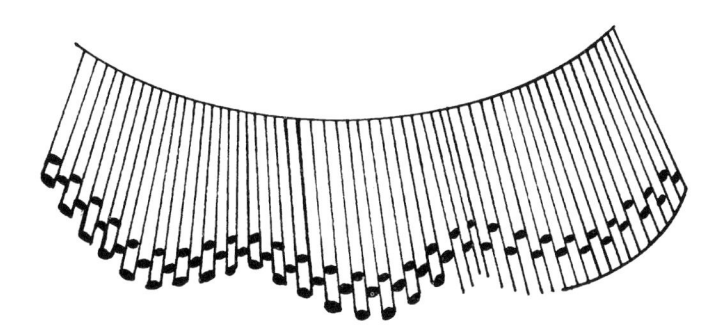

Figure 4b

Trouble Shooting

1. Deal with all breakages as they occur.

2. Never over dampen your iced bridge. It is better to take longer to remove it than to try speeding up the process by over wetting. If too much water is used it begins to creep up the dropped strings as well as the bridge line causing part of the strings to melt away with the bridge. These will then need re-piping.

3. If a single string should break and the bridge is still in place, remove it by painting it gently with a little water until it becomes soft. The top can be scratched off with the aid of a sharp pin or the point of a fine pair of scissors. Re-pipe the string carefully.

4. If more than one string has broken and the bridge is still in place gently dampen the broken strings and ease these away. Scratch away any tops of the strings which are left attached to the cake. Pipe the strings back into place taking care to pipe one string at a time and making sure each is dry before piping the next.

If the bridge has been removed, pipe a false bridge in the gap. Using a no.0 piping tube, pipe a line of icing using either the ends of the dropped strings, or if you have joined these with dots use the dots as supports. Leave this bridge to dry for 30 minutes then pipe the dropped strings. (see figure 1)

5. If a large section of the extension work breaks you will need to pipe a new section of bridge and join this to either edge of the unbroken section. Knock out any partially broken strings and insert one or two brackets into the gap created. Place the new bridge on top. Join the ends to adjacent dots with softened royal icing and leave to dry. Remove the brackets and fill in the section with dropped strings. Finish in the original pattern of dots, etc.

6. If the piping tube blocks frequently, re-sieve the royal icing or sieve the icing sugar through two pieces of butter muslin before making the royal icing.

7. If the strings break repeatedly this often means that your royal icing is too soft and stretches after you have finished piping the dropped string. Watch the top of the string after you have piped it. If you can see it moving and it becomes thinner at one point or another you need to stiffen your icing. You may also have large air bubbles in the icing which often cause strings to break. In this instance the break will appear as if a knife has cut through the string. To help cure this problem leave the icing overnight before using it for piping.

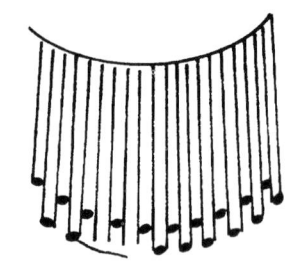

Figure 1

Embroidery and Lace

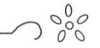

Embroidery and lace can be used for a variety of different reasons from enhancing your extension work to covering up mistakes. Whatever your needs always use the finest piping tubes 0 or 00. Embroidery may consist of fine lines, scallops, flowers, leaves, etc.

To pipe a flower

Fill a piping bag with some softly peaking royal icing and a no. 0 piping tube and pipe a dot of icing onto the cake's surface. Stop pressing on the bag and pull back sharply, just above the cake's surface and horizontal to it. This will leave a thin tail. Repeat this procedure evenly in a small circle ensuring the top and bottom piped petals are slightly longer. Make a dot in the centre. (see figure 1)

Leaves are piped as single petals and tend to be used on their own or in groups of two or three arranged along a stem. (see figure 2)

Small flowers can be made by piping five small dots in a circle and adding one in the centre. Arranged with leaves they look most attractive. (see figure 3)

Bows can also be piped with fine piping tubes and look very dainty when piped directly onto the dropped strings. For a bow, pipe a continuous line of icing following the arrows. (see figure 4)

Monograms, hearts, flowers, etc. can all be piped onto the dropped extension work strings. Always use a slightly softer icing for this and take great care not to touch the strings with your tube. Use a fine, pointed paintbrush to finish your embroidery.

Lace

Lace can be piped directly onto the top of the extension work (poor man's lace) or in small sections (lace off-pieces) which are attached separately.

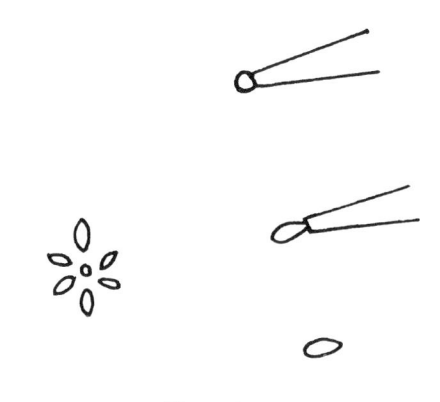

Figure 1

Figure 2

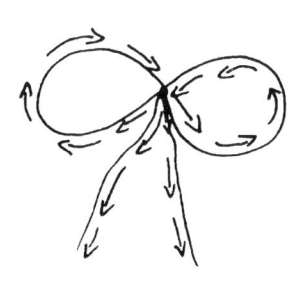

Figure 4

Figure 3

Poor Man's Lace

Poor Man's Lace is piped directly onto the top of the extension work. It is one of the simplest forms of decorative finishes and is built up in layers. Begin by piping a complete ring of small even curves around the top. Gently lift each curve with a damp paintbrush to allow it to stand away from the dropped strings.

Pipe a second series of loops, the points of which touch the centre of the loop of the preceeding layer. (see figure 1)

Pipe a third series of loops. (see figure 2)

A small dot can be piped on the top of the final loops if wished. (see figure 2)

Dots may also be piped where the points of the loops touch the cake. (see figure 3)

> **Handy tip**
>
> Always use the same size piping tube for your lace as you have used for the dropped strings. Normally this will be a no. 0 or 00. Neaten all rough areas with a fine paintbrush.

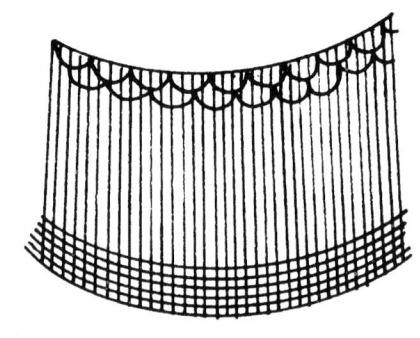

Figure 1

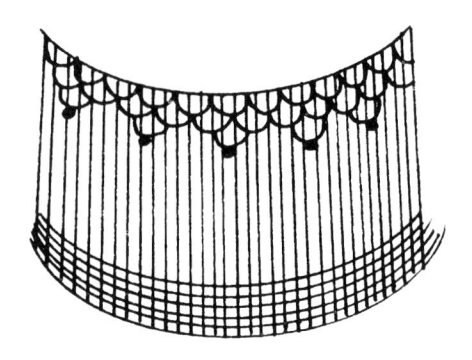

Figure 2

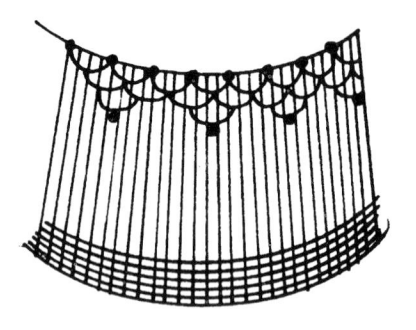

Figure 3

Lace off-pieces

Small pieces of lace attached to extension work look very dainty and are well worth the time it takes to make.

Pipe lace pieces using the same size tube as you used to pipe the extension work dropped strings. Neaten all rough areas with a fine paintbrush.

1. Bring your royal icing to peaking consistency and sieve it through butter muslin. Fill a piping bag with some sieved icing and a no. 0 or 00 piping tube.

2. Place your lace pattern under cellophane on a stiff board and tape down the sides. Pipe each piece of lace and leave to dry for 15 minutes. (see figure 1)

Lace looks especially lovely on the top edge of coloured extension work if part of it is coloured with powder to match the deeper extension work bridge. Always powder the lace before it is removed from the cellophane and work well away from the cake when doing this. (see figure 2) Take a paintbrush and brush a little powder over the area of lace to be coloured then blow away the excess colour with a puffer. Remove the lace from the cellophane and set aside. Attach this lace to the cake in groups ensuring no particles of the powder are allowed to come into contact with the cake's surface.

Attaching lace to the cake

1. Using the first finger of each hand, gently run your two fingers between the rows of lace pieces. Ensure that you form a ridge of cellophane which will move under the lace, lifting each piece and freeing it to a greater or lesser degree.

2. Gently move your crank handled palette knife under the pieces of lace to free them. Lift one onto the blade with the aid of a fine paintbrush. (see figure 3)

3. Bring the palette knife to the cake. Pipe a small dot or couple of dots of soft royal icing onto the cake.

4. Gently slide the lace piece off the palette knife onto the soft dots. Use a paintbrush to gently ease it into position. (see figure 4)

> ### Handy tip
> Care must be taken to ensure that the palette knife does not come into contact with the extension work lines.

Figure 1

Figure 2

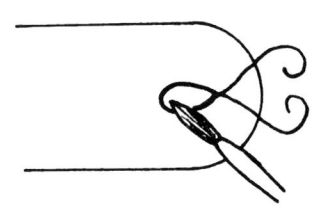

Figure 3

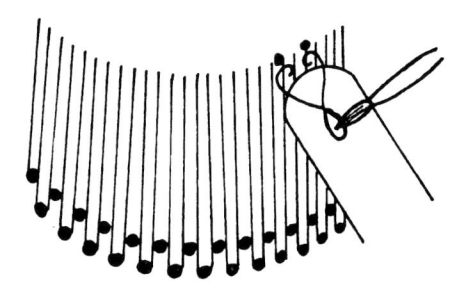

Figure 4

Variations on a Theme

There are many different designs you can pipe using fixed and floating extension work. As you become more experienced, try experimenting using a mixture of the techniques described and incorporating your own ideas.

Working with a different shaped top edge on your extension work can lend interest to the finished piece without making it too complicated to complete. Some of the cakes in this book have been worked using different styles of top edge. Once you have scored your top edge onto the cake and completed the bridge, pipe the dropped strings from this scored edge onto the bridge.

Always remember that whatever pattern you use it must balance with the rest of your design. For example it is no good deciding to have one curved top edge to every three bridge curves if you have ten bridge curves. You will have one left over.

Fixed Extension Work

Using ribbon inserts

Ribbon inserts enable you to carry a colour from the top of the cake through your design in an attractive and simple fashion. Happy Birthday featured on page 71 is a fine example of this technique.

1. First mark your pattern and pipe the bridge.

2. Measure the depth 'D' of the proposed extension work from the top edge to the bridge.

3. Cut lengths of ribbon using the above measurement as a guide. 3mm ($^1/_8$") wide ribbon is ideal for this.

4. Touch a small dot of icing to the top edge of the proposed extension work and press one of the pieces of ribbon onto this.

5. Let the ribbon fall until it rests vertically onto the bridge. It should just fit. (see figure 1)

6. Touch a dot of icing to the bridge directly beneath the ribbon and press into place.

7. Before attaching the ribbon a small "V" can be cut into the base to give a neater effect to the points of a curve.

8. Pipe the first string as close to the ribbon insert as possible working as before until you have filled in the gap. (see figure 2) Piped lace may be inserted in place of the ribbon using the same technique.

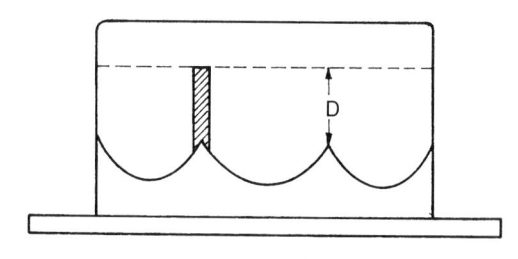

Figure 1

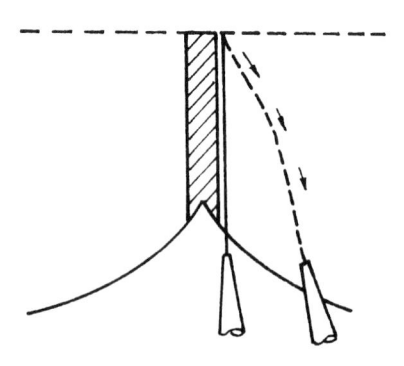

Figure 2

Working on a shaped bridge

This technique is most suited to curved bridge patterns as it requires the bridge to be shaped in sections.

1. Mark the pattern for your extension work onto the cake.

2. Fill a bag with royal icing and a no. 1 piping tube. Pipe one continuous curved line following the pattern curves.

3. Always work on one curve at a time. Pipe a second line just short of the first at both ends. Take a damp paintbrush and smooth both ends flat. (see figure 1)

4. Pipe a third line just short of the second and continue in this way shortening each successive line until eight rows in all have been piped. (see figure 2)

Neaten each row with a paintbrush thus forming a neat curve with no areas of daylight showing through.

5. Pipe one continuous line around the bridge to finish. (see figure 3)

6. Fill a piping bag with royal icing and a no. 0 or 00 piping tube.

Pipe dropped strings beginning at one side of the bridge and continuing to the other. Ensure all the strings are as straight and even as possible.

Figure 1

Figure 2

Figure 3

Enhancing corners

When piping extension work on a square cake it is often useful to be able to make a feature of the shape. This technique is ideal for the purpose.

1. Mark your pattern onto the cake's side.

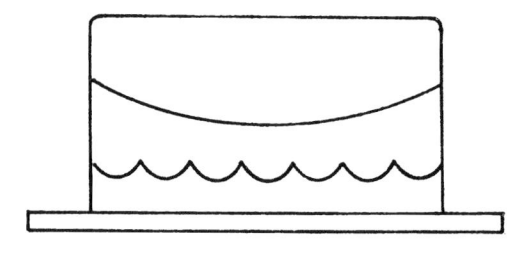

Handy tip

If you are working on a curved bridge ensure that the centre of one curve lies against the centre of the cake's pointed side corner. Try raising the top edge of the extension work at the corners then gently curving them down to a low point in the centre of each side. (see figure 1)

Figure 1

2. Pipe four continuous bridge lines around the cake's sides.

3. Overpipe two bridge lines, beginning either side of one or two central curves on the cake's side. (see figure 2)

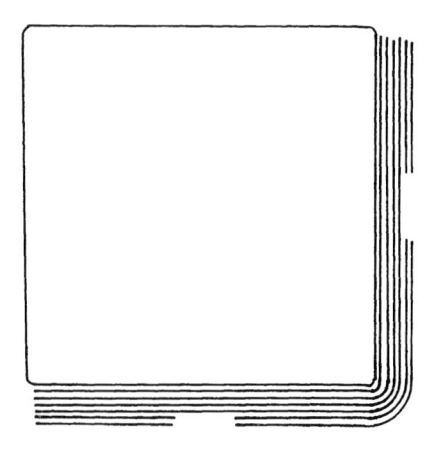

4. Overpipe two bridge lines, beginning either side of three or four central curves on the cake's side. (see figure 3) If you have allowed for one curve in step three allow for three curves here. If two allow 4 here.

5. Overpipe two bridge lines beginning either side of five or six central curves on the cake's side.

6. Continue in this way until you have a maximum of twelve bridge lines at the corner. Leave to dry thoroughly then pipe your dropped strings.

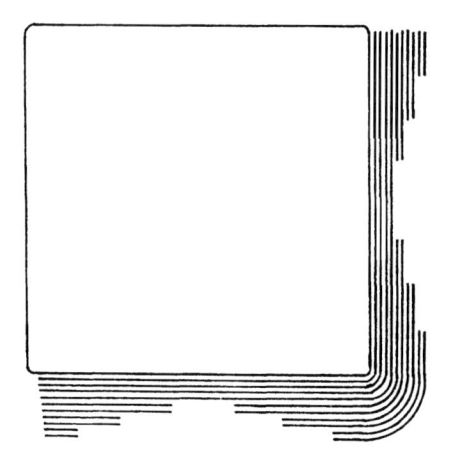

Figure 2

Figure 3

The following techniques should only be attempted when you are thoroughly confident with piping extension work. The different decorative styles are listed in increasing skill level thus enabling you to decide the degree of difficulty you feel confident to attempt.

Double extension work

This looks particularly attractive if worked on a coloured bridge with darker strings forming the background and paler strings the foreground.

1. Mark your pattern onto the cake. Colour enough royal icing to pipe all of your bridge and approximately half of the dropped strings.

2. Using some coloured icing and a no. 1 piping tube pipe a bridge 6 lines deep. (see figure 1)

3. In a separate container place enough coloured icing to complete a further 5 lines. Place the remaining coloured icing in a bowl. Add ½ as much white royal icing, set aside and mark this bowl (1).

Mix the icing thoroughly, sieve and place some icing into a bag fitted with a no. 0 or 00 piping tube.

4. Pipe a continuous line of extension work around the cake side. (see figure 2)

5. Add 4 more bridge lines using the reserved icing. (see figure 3)

6. Mix icing (1) with ½ as much white royal icing.

Mix the icing thoroughly, sieve and place some icing into a bag fitted with a no. 0 or 00 piping tube.

7. Pipe a second continuous line of extension work around the cake side. (see figure 4)

8. Finish with lace pieces if desired.

Figure 1

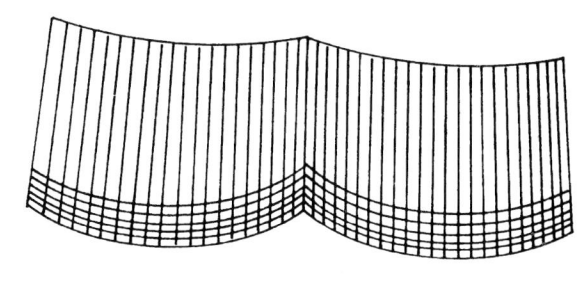

Figure 2

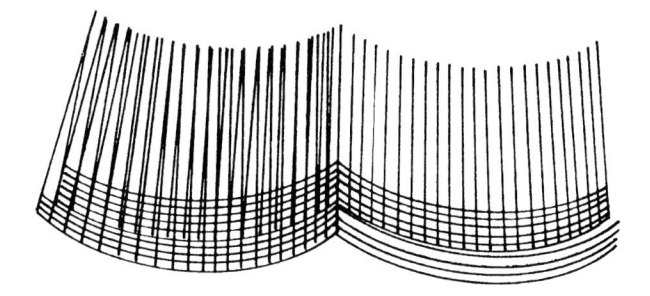

Figure 4

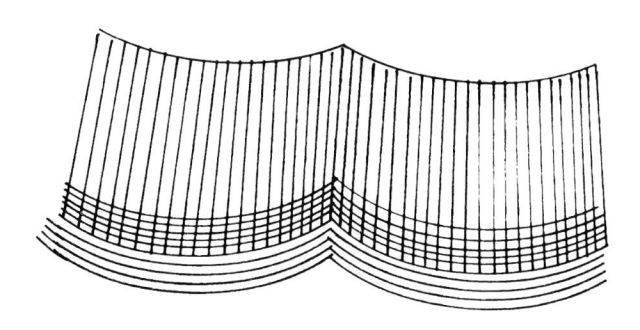

Figure 3

Double extension work with open panels

Small panels decorated with lace, coloured dots, or flowers can look most attractive if interspaced with areas of double extension work. Heart's Delight is a fine example of this technique and is featured on page 17.

1. Mark your pattern onto the cake and pipe the first layer of extension work, following the instructions given for double extension work, steps 1 - 5. (see figure 1)

2. Mix icing (1) with ½ as much white royal icing. Mix the icing thoroughly, sieve and place some icing into a bag fitted with a no. 0 or 00 piping tube.

3. Pipe a second layer of extension work, filling each alternate curve. (see figure 2) The gaps left can now be filled. A small rosebud attached to the base of each gap and framed by slanting strings can look very pretty. (see figure 3) Small dots of icing may be piped directly onto the strings to further enhance the design. These dots are known as hailspots.

Figure 1

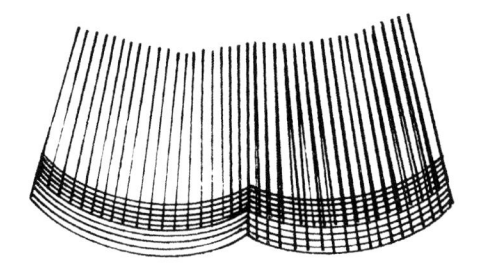

Figure 2

Figure 3

Extension work using slanting strings

This form of decoration is very attractive if piped as the outer row in double extension work. It benefits from having a slightly deeper background layer as this helps to show off the pattern of paler slanted strings, etc. Try to work on a curved bridge if possible. You can then decide how you want the slanting pattern to work.

An example of this type of extension work can be seen on Congratulations featured on page 81.

1. Mark your pattern onto the cake and pipe the first layer of extension work following the instructions for double extension work, steps 1-5.

2. Sieve the icing and place some into a bag fitted with a number 0 or 00 piping tube. Pipe a second layer of dropped strings, slanting the first string and carefully following this slant as you progress around the cake. (see figure 1)

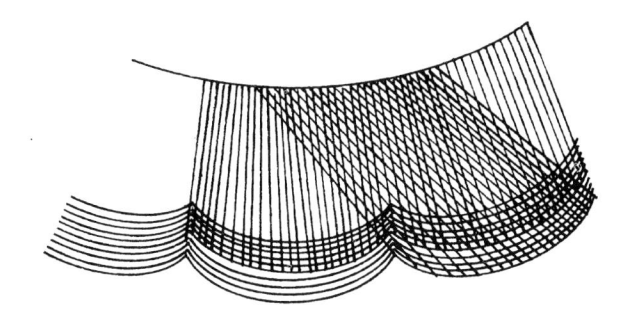

Figure 1

Handy tip
Check your slanting strings every 25mm (1") and adjust the angle of slant if necessary.

The first layer of extension work can also be piped on the slant. It is a good idea to slant this in the opposite direction, thus enabling light to throw shadow onto the work and enhance the overall appearance of the design. (see figure 2)

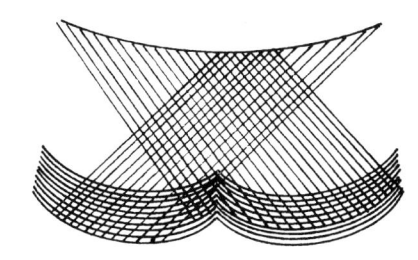

Figure 2

Tiered Extension Work

This form of decoration consists of tiers of extension work piped as a feature on the cake. The tiers look particularly attractive on Oval or Heart shaped cakes where they can be used to enhance the shape. A pattern showing the exact location of the tiers needs to be carefully prepared and marked onto the cake before you start to pipe any of the decorative work.

1. Mark your pattern onto the cake. (see figure 1)

2. Pipe the first tier of extension work.

3. Pipe a second bridge immediately above the top of the dropped strings of the first tier. Do not touch the first row of strings with your new bridge as this may cause them to break. (see figure 2)

> ### Handy tip
> When piping this bridge use a paintbrush to gently taper the ends in towards the cake. This will give a neater finish to the work and makes it easier to attach any decorative finish.

4. Pipe a second tier of dropped strings onto this new bridge. (see figure 3)

If you are planning to pipe more than two tiers of extension work as a single feature on the cake, try to bring the finished work to a point. This ensures the work will not look too heavy when completed.

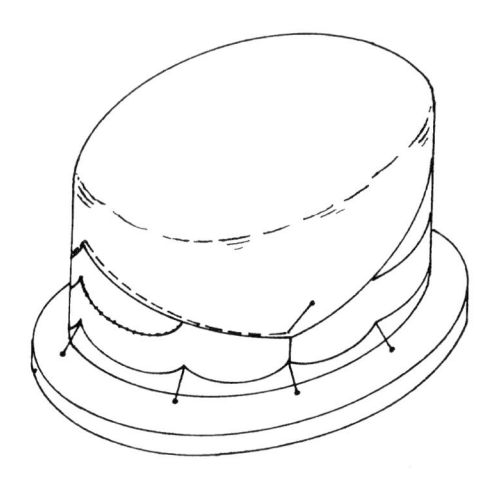

Figure 1

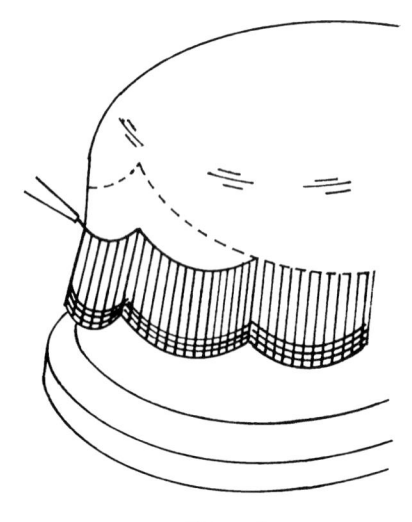

Figure 2

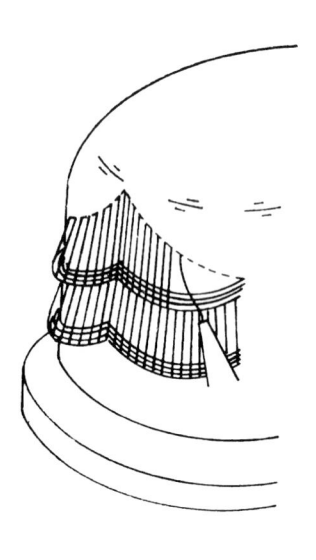

Figure 3

Extension work on an upside down bridge

It will be necessary for the cake to be covered with sugarpaste at least one week before you can begin this decorative technique.

At first it may seem quite daunting to turn a cake upside down to work but do not worry. By now you should feel confident enough to tackle it.

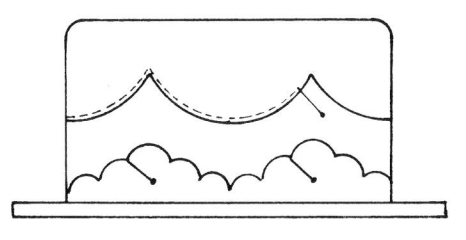

1. Mark your pattern onto the cake.

> **Handy tip**
> The finished bridge looks particularly attractive if worked on a graduated curve. (see figure 1)

Figure 1

2. Prepare the cake for piping the bridge. First place a piece of foam on top of the cake making sure you leave a border of 25mm (1") between the edge of the foam and the edge of the cake.

3. Place your turntable in a good light. Find something, which when placed on top of the turntable will bring your cake to a good working height and place it on top.

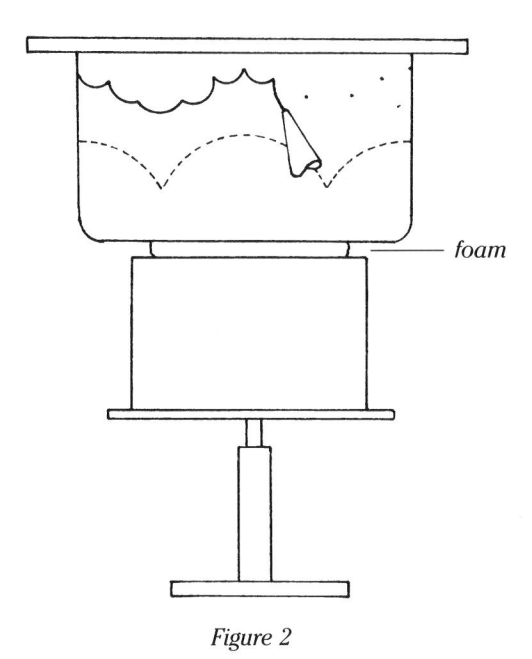

> **Handy tip**
> I find my icing container or workbox are ideal for this.

4. Invert the cake onto this support. Always ensure your cake is firm before you commence working on it.

5. Pipe the bridge as before, noting that the loops will hang upside down. (see figure 2) Make sure there are no gaps between the bridge loops.

6. Leave the bridge to dry for one hour then turn the cake right way up again placing it back onto the support. Pipe the dropped strings to the upside down bridge. (see figure 3)

7. Finish the top with lace if desired.

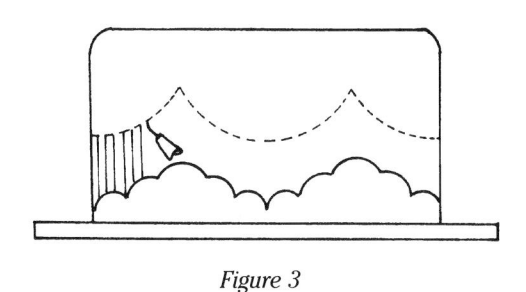

Figure 2

Figure 3

Floating Extension Work

Double Extension Work

1. Mark the cake with your pattern.

2. Make your bridge pattern. You will need to make this pattern with two floating bridge lines, one being 25mm (1") larger than the other.

To do this complete steps 1-7 of the floating bridge pattern section but do not cut the pattern section at this stage.

Draw a new circle 25mm (1") larger than circle S. Mark this K.

Draw a second circle of curves, the points of each touching S and the centre of each, touching circle K. (see figure 1)

3. Pipe bridge 1 and complete the first layer of floating extension work.

4. Pipe bridge 2. Replace the brackets around the cake taking care not to damage the first layer of floating extension work. These brackets should be assembled to rest 3mm (1/8") lower than the top edge of the first layer. Assemble the new bridge on top. (see figure 2)

Leave a gap of 9mm (3/8") between the original floating extension work layer and the points of this second bridge. Take care to line up the points of the first and second layer of work before progressing to pipe any anchor strings.

5. Pipe the second layer of floating extension work to the new bridge. (see figure 3)

6. Remove this bridge and finish with a double row of dots. Add lace and hailspots if desired.

Figure 1

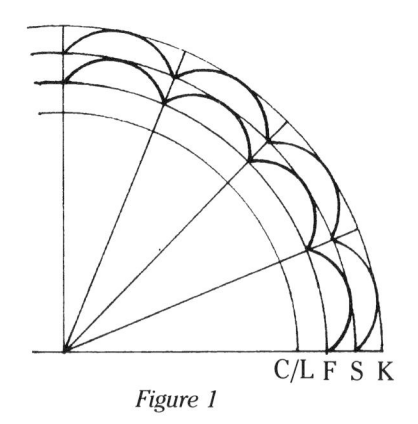

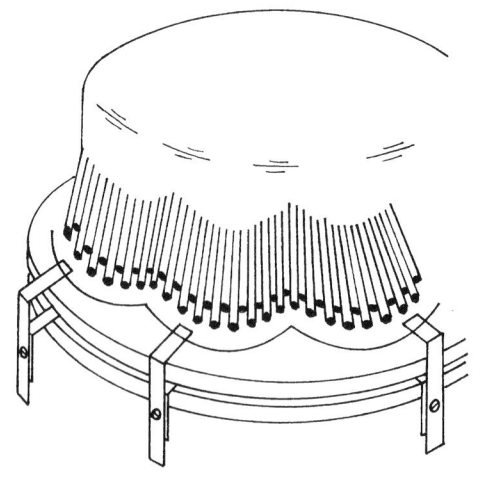

Figure 2

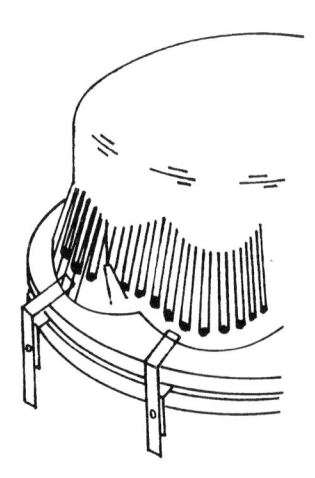

Figure 3

Tiered with a double skirt

This decoration requires great skill and patience, particularly if you intend piping a double layer of floating extension work as your bottom tier. It looks lovely if embroidery is piped on the first layer and hailspots are piped at intervals on the second layer.

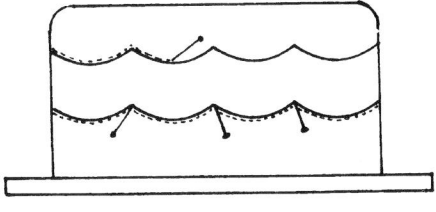

1. Mark your pattern onto the cake. (see figure 1)

2. Make your pattern for the floating bridge as described in the section on floating double extension work.

3. Pipe the first bridge and leave to dry for 15 minutes.

4. Arrange the brackets around the cake, assemble the bridge and pipe the first layer of floating extension work. Remove the bridge and complete the bottom edge.

5. Pipe any embroidery on the strings. (see figure 2)

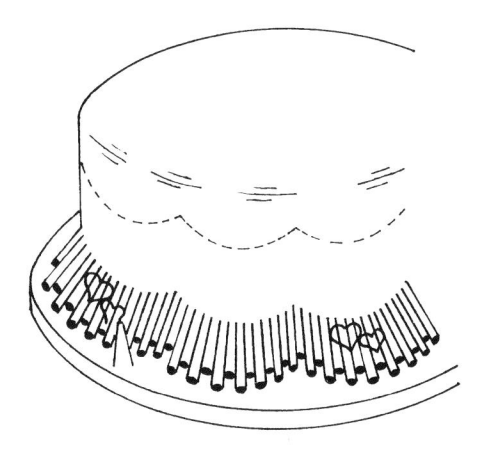

6. Pipe the second bridge and leave to dry for 15 minutes.

7. Arrange the brackets around the cake, taking care not to touch the first layer. Assemble the bridge ensuring it is evenly spaced around the cake.

Figure 1

Figure 2

Handy tip

Make sure all the curves are lined up or off-set around the cake. Pipe stops to secure the second bridge before beginning to pipe the dropped strings. Remove every other bracket as soon as the anchor strings are dry.

8. Pipe the second layer of dropped strings. Remove the bridge and finish the strings with dots.

9. Repipe the first bridge and leave to dry for 15 minutes.

10. Assemble the brackets around the cake to allow the new bridge to rest 6mm (¹/₄") below the top of the first layer. (see figure 3) Take great care that you do not damage this first layer when rearranging these brackets. Place the bridge on top.

11. Pipe the dropped strings onto this bridge, removing any damaged areas as you work. You will need to take care that you do not move the brackets while you work.

12. Pipe a line of graduated dots following each curve of the bridge. Remove the bridge taking extreme care and repairing any damage at once.

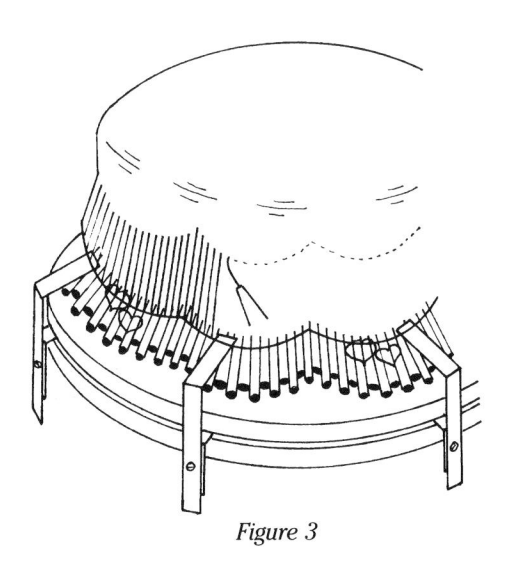

Finish with lace and embroidery if desired.

Figure 3

Double with inserts

This technique looks especially pretty if piped on an engagement or wedding cake. It consists of a double layer of floating extension work with hearts, flowers or wedding rings piped in "windows" around the cakes sides. It is featured on Golden Showers, page 52 and 53.

1. Make your pattern and mark this onto your cake.

2. Complete one row of floating extension work following the instructions given for floating extension work on a continuous bridge.

3. Pipe a small area of embroidery on every other curved section.

4. Pipe a second bridge and complete a second layer of floating extension work over the first, following steps 3 - 6 of the instructions for double extension work.

5. Pipe dots joining each pair of strings to form a window over the embroidered layer. (see figure 1)

6. Using a fine paintbrush, dampen the individual strings inside this window and remove each with care. The embroidery should show through the cleared area. (see figure 2)

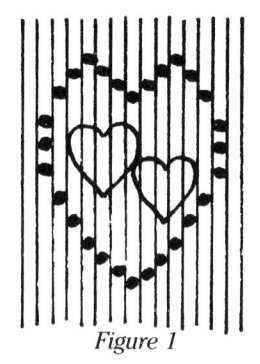

Figure 1

Figure 2

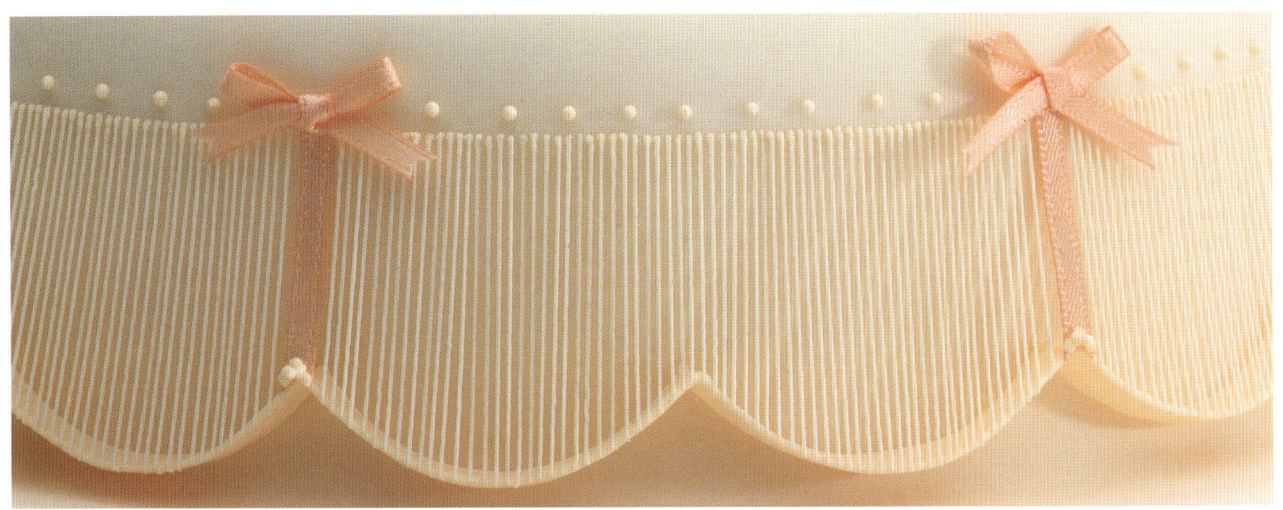

Happy Birthday
Decorated by Gill Martin

Kentish Scene

On an inverted bridge

This looks very attractive if used as a canopy over flowers, pictures, etc. It is a very skilful technique and requires practise to perfect and is featured on Kentish Scene page 72.

1. Make your pattern for the cake's side and mark this onto the cake.

2. Make the pattern for the inverted bridge.

    (a) Measure the diameter of the cake, add 25mm (1") and divide by two. Using a pair of compasses opened to this size, draw a circle onto a piece of paper.

    (b) Using a protractor divide the circle into 12, 16 etc.

    (c) Using one segment, find the centre by drawing a straight line connecting points A and B. Measure this line and divide in half. Mark this point C.

    (d) Draw a half circle AB, using C as the centre. (see figure 1)

3. Place the pattern under cellophane and pipe each bridge scallop separately.

4. Assemble two brackets, placing them in front of one inscribed curve on the cake's side. Make sure the points of the piped bridge curve will rest on the brackets.

5. Place a long glass headed pin into the cake at the central point of the inscribed curve. Angle this pin down. (see figure 2)

6. Gently lay one curve over the pin, allowing each of its points to rest on a bracket. Repeat with the other curves, ensuring they are equidistant from the cake. Add stops where necessary. (see figure 3)

7. Using a slightly softer royal icing, join the points together.

> **Handy tip**
>
> You may find it easier to work with the bridge joined in four quarters rather than trying to join all the points at once.

8. Using a slightly stiffer royal icing and no. 00 piping tube, pipe the dropped strings.

9. Remove the bridge and finish with dots. Add lace off-pieces or poor man's lace if desired.

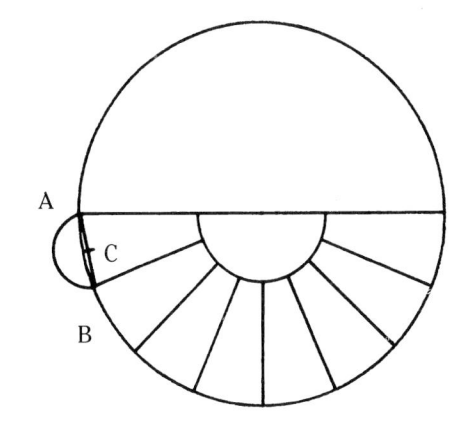

Figure 1

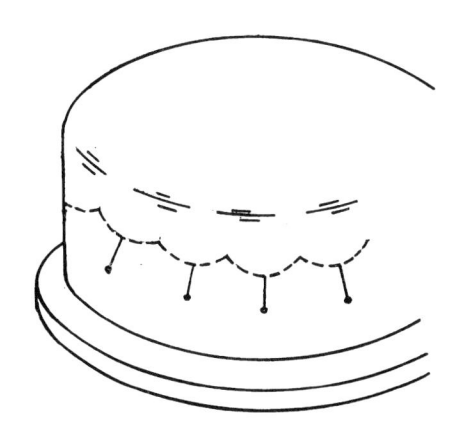

Figure 2

Figure 3

Cake Designs

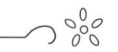

The following pages give details on how to complete the cakes featured in the colour plates. Beginning with the easiest, Christmas Time and progressing through increasing levels of skill to the most intricate True Love.

Each description includes details of necessary equipment and the sections in the book relevant to the design. Before you begin to work find each of these sections and mark them with small pieces of paper for ease of reference.

You will need the following equipment for all of the cakes described:-
adding machine roll, pencil, ruler, pins, sellotape, pair of compasses, royal icing, greaseproof piping bags, piping tubes 1,0, paintbrush no.1.0, greaseproof paper, cellophane, firm surface for piping lace. "L" brackets will be needed for all floating extension work designs. Any additional equipment you may need is included under each cake description.

Cakes

Christmas Time

Happy Birthday

Congratulations

Hearts Delight

Merry Christmas

Lullaby

Castle in the Air

Cream Sensation

Best of Friends

Golden Showers

Kentish Scene

True Love

Christmas Time

This lovely example of a Christmas cake comprises of simple panels of fixed bridge extension work and lace holly wreaths. It would look lovely as the centrepiece of a christmas celebration. It is featured on page 18.

Additional equipment
200mm (8") round cake on an 275mm (11") cake drum both covered with white sugarpaste
Food colours: Paste - christmas red, mint green, cream, dark brown

Find the following sections in the book
Pressure piped run-outs   page 33
Pattern making for fixed extension work   page 21
Fixed extension work   page 41

To decorate the cake

1. Trace the pattern, and prick it out onto the cake top. Care should be taken to ensure the pattern is placed in the centre. To do this place the pattern on top centering it by using a ruler to measure from the cake's edge to the pattern and continuing around the design.

2. Follow the instructions given for pressure piped run-outs, and pipe the picture on top of the cake. Pipe the message.

3. Follow the instructions for pattern making to construct your side pattern ensuring you have 24 deep scallops with a straight heading.

4. Mark the points of the curves onto your sugarpaste covered cake. Use a no.1 piping tube and royal icing which is just off peak to pipe the bridge in groups of three scallops with one scallops left clear between each group.

5. Pipe your dropped strings onto this bridge, removing the ends with a damp paintbrush.

6. Follow the instructions given for piping lace to trace and pipe your lace pieces. Attach these above the points on the scallops. Pipe the Holly Wreaths and leave to dry for one hour.

7. Remove from the cellophane. Carefully attach these pieces with small dots of royal icing in the gaps between the groups of extension work strings. Take care to overlap the extension work slightly. Support with brackets until dry. (see figure 1) Pipe small dots evenly around the outer edge of the sugarpaste cake drum to finish.

Handy Tip
It will look neater if you gently brush both ends of each bridge line to shape them into the cake side. Pipe ten bridge lines.

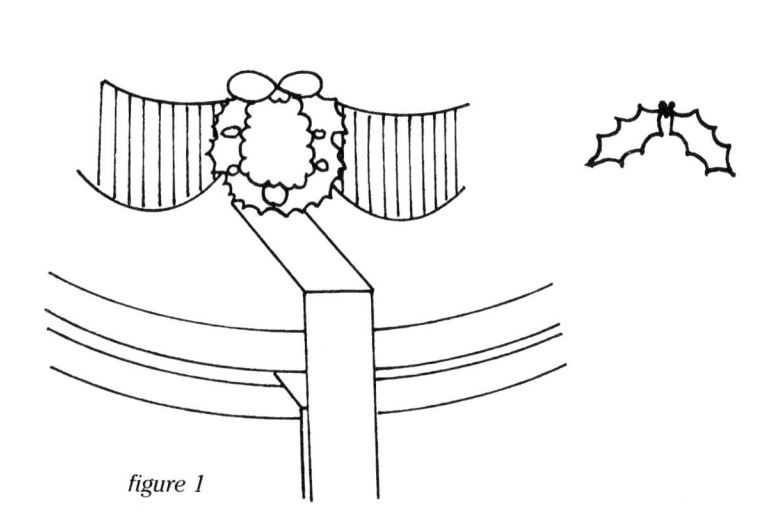

figure 1

Happy Birthday

This delightful cake would surely please any little lady on her birthday. It consists of a bas relief picture and extension work with ribbon inserts. It is featured on page 71.

Additional equipment
200mm (8") round cake covered with marzipan on an 275mm (11") cake drum
3mm (1/8") peach ribbon
Food colours: Paste - peach, dark brown, black, mulberry, paprika

Find the following sections in the book
Pressure piped run-outs   page 33
Fixed extension work using ribbon inserts   page 60
Pattern making for fixed extension work   page 21

To decorate the cake

1. Cover the cake and drum with peach sugarpaste. Mark a border on the edge of the cake drum using one side of a pair of crimpers and impressing it into the sugarpaste. Continue round the side until the design is complete.

2. Follow the section on pattern making to make the pattern for the cake side. This cake has 16 sections. Mark this onto the cake.

3. Trace the pattern for the bas relief and work this on top of the cake. To do this:

   (a) Inscribe the girl's face, hands, socks, and shoes onto the cake together with the bird.

   (b) Cut out the bird's wings and letter from a thin sheet of pastillage. To make pastillage follow the recipe given.

   (c) Pressure pipe the face, hands, socks and shoes onto the cake. Pressure pipe the bird and insert the bird's wing. Support this with a small piece of foam until dry.

   (d) Mix some sugarpaste and pastillage together in the proportion of two parts sugarpaste to one part pastillage.

   (e) Roll out and cut into thin strips then frill them. Dampen the cake and lay the frills on top. Ensure the first just overlaps the top of the socks.

   (f) Roll out and place your traced pattern on top. Cut around the dress, allowing 12mm (1/2") extra around the sides. Dampen the cake and lay this dress on top. Ensure the top fits against the neck. Arrange the dress into folds.

   (g) Mould some sugarpaste into an arm and cover with a thin layer of the sugarpaste and pastillage mixture.

   (h) Add piped dots and ribbon. Write a message on the pastillage letter and attach this to the cake. Pipe the bird's feet, just over the edge of the letter.

4. Following the instructions given for extension work with ribbon inserts, cut small pieces of 3mm (1/8") peach ribbon to fit from the bridge to the top edge of the proposed dropped strings. Attach these to the cake and pipe the dropped strings.

5. Pipe a row of evenly spaced dots above the extension work and attach ribbon bows above the ribbon inserts.

6. Pipe a line of dots on top of the crimper line on the sugarpaste cake drum.

Recipe for Pastillage

Ingredients - teaspoon used 5mls

1 1/2 level tsp gelatine } soak for 30 minutes
4 dessert spoons cold water

450 gms (1lb) icing sugar

1/2 level tsp gum tragacanth

Method:

Place the icing sugar and gum tragacanth in an ovenproof bowl, cover and place in the oven for 20 minutes, gas mark 1, 100°C.

Place the gelatine and water mixture over a pan of hot water until dissolved then add to the warmed icing sugar and mix well. Knead until smooth.

Congratulations

A heart shapedd caked covered in sparkling white sugarpaste and crowned with an enchanting arrangement of favourite flowers, make the celebration even more special. This cake is featured on page 81.

The extension work, comprises a deep pink bridge with a double row of dropped strings. The underskirt is piped in a lighter shade with the top layer combining groups of slanted and straight dropped strings.

Additional equipment
200mm (8") heart shaped cake on an 275mm (11") cake drum both covered with white sugarpaste
3mm (1/8") deep pink ribbon
Food colours: Paste - cyclamen pink,
            silver
spray of flowers.

Find the following sections in the book
Double extension work on a fixed bridge   page 63
Lace   page 57
Pattern making for fixed extension work   page 21

To decorate the cake

1. Cover the cake and board at least 24 hours before decorating. Follow the section on pattern making fixed bridge, to make the pattern for the cake side. This cake has 16 sections. Mark this onto the cake.

2. Cut the pattern in half, joining it to allow the centre of one curve to fit against the point of the heart. Mark the pattern onto the cake.

3. Fix a narrow band of ribbon around the base of the cake. Attach it to the back where the join will not show as much. To do this:

   (a) Place a pin through the ribbon and push this into the sugarpaste. Leave 25mm (1") of the ribbon free. Pipe a short line of icing and stick the free end of the ribbon down.

   (b) Wrap the ribbon around the cake piping small lines of icing at intervals of approximately 100mm (4"). Make sure the ribbon lies against these and is level.

   (c) Anchor the ribbon with another pin 25mm (1") short of the end. Fix this end with a little icing. Overlap the two ends slightly.

   (d) Remove the pins by carefully pulling them out one at a time. Hold the ends of the ribbon firmly against the cake whilst doing this.

   (e) Pipe a row of even dots along the ribbon.

4. Follow the section on double extension work and pipe the first row of dropped strings and the second bridge.

5. Pipe the second layer of extension work starting in the centre front with 5 straight dropped strings. Follow the pattern to ensure you pipe this layer in the correct order. Pipe one side at a time reversing the pattern for the second side.

6. Use a no.1 piping tube and the same shade of icing to pipe a continuous line around the bottom edge of the extension work. Finish with two graduated loops on the points.

7. Add a spray of flowers and pipe your message in white royal icing.

8. Pipe pairs of wings and tails for the birds on cellophane, using pale blue icing and a no.00 piping tube. Leave to dry. Using a no.2 piping tube and pale blue icing pipe the birds and immediately insert the wings and tail. Use a no.0 piping tube and white royal icing to pipe from the cake over one bird's beak, the message and the second bird's beak finishing on the cake. Tip the bird's wings and paint the message with silver.

9. Using a no1 piping tube, pipe a snail's trail around the outer edge of the sugarpaste on the cake drum.

10. Following the section on lace, pipe and attach lace off-pieces to the top edge of the extension work.

11. Following the pattern pipe the embroidery freehand above the extension work.

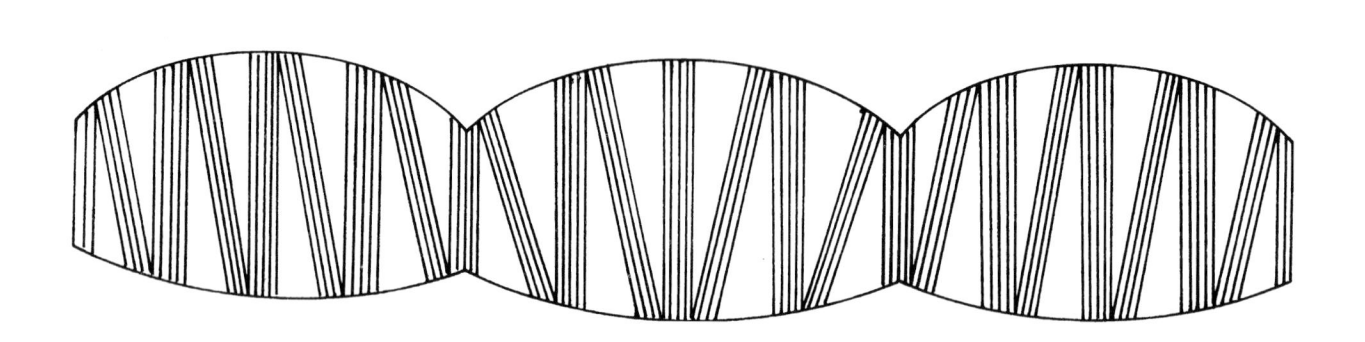

Congratulations

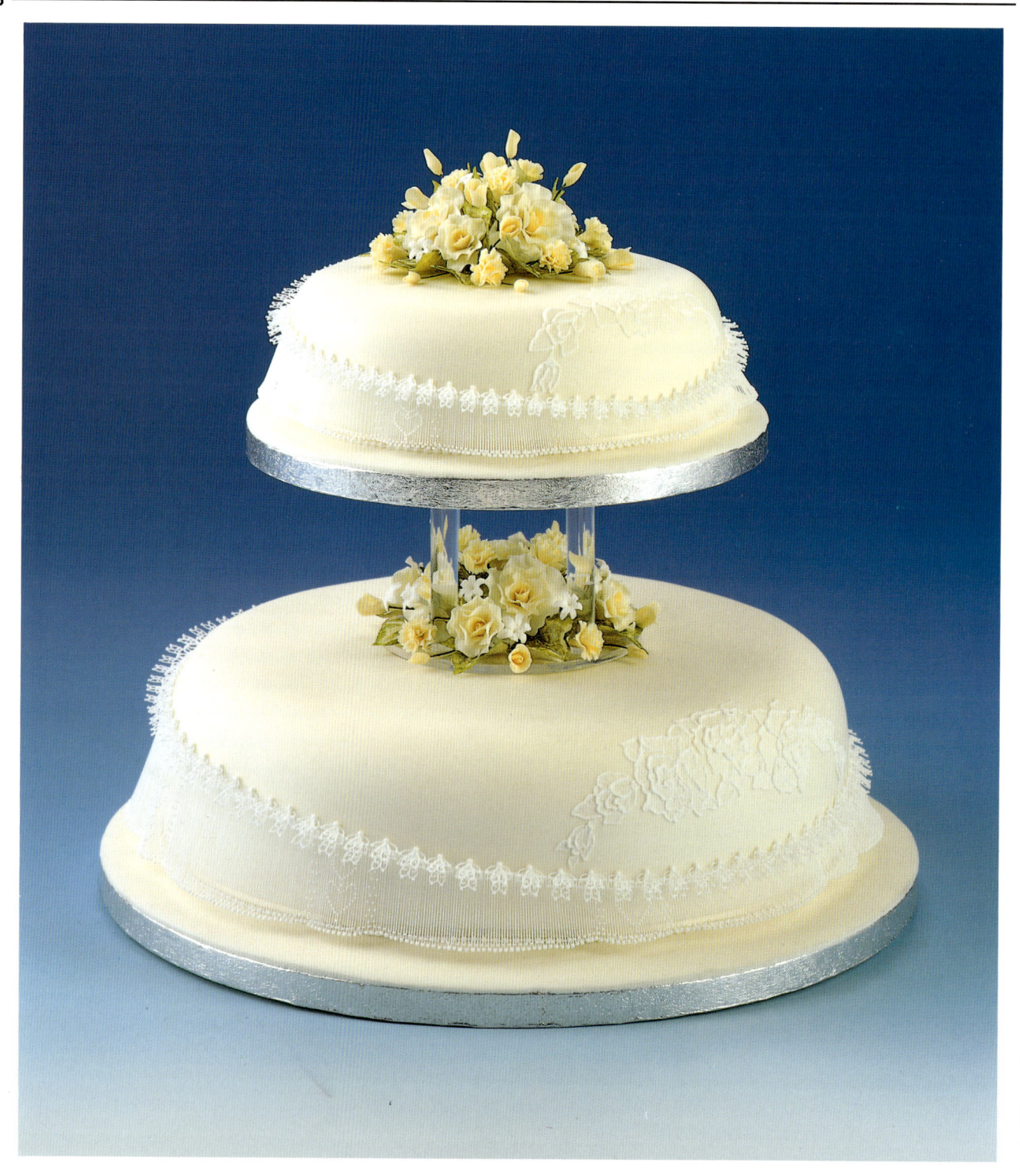

Cream Sensation

Cream Sensation

True Love
Took third place - Open Masterclass at the London Christmas Exhibition 1990

Heart's Delight

This delicate cake is a fine example of double extension work with open panels, featuring open roses, gold edged ribbon and white blossoms. It would be perfect for a first anniversary or an engagement celebration. This cake is featured on page 17.

Additional equipment

150mm (6") heart shaped cake on a 225mm (9") cake drum both covered with white sugarpaste
3mm (1/8") gold edged ribbon
12mm (1/2") pale pink ribbon
Food colours: Liquid - rose pink   Paste - gooseberry
                Powder - candy pink
2 full blown open roses
17 wired anonymous flowers
8 unwired anonymous flowers
24 stamens with very small heads

Find the following sections in the book

Double extension work with open panels	page 64
Lace	page 57
Pattern making for fixed extension work	page 21

To decorate the cake

1. Follow the section, pattern making for fixed extension work, to make the pattern for the cake side. This cake has 16 sections. Inscribe this onto the cake making sure that the centre of one scallop is in line with the point of the heart.

2. Colour some sugarpaste pale pink and roll out a thin strip. Using a knife cut this into a long thin strip about 3mm (1/8") wide. Dampen the bottom edge of the cake and attach this strip.

3. Using a no.1 piping tube, pipe a snail's trail around the lower edge of the sugarpaste strip.

4. Roll out and cut a thin strip of pale pink sugarpaste. Attach this in small pieces of equal width and length to the cake side approximately 6mm (1/4") above the straight inscribed line.

Prick the top and bottom edges of each piece with a round beaded pin or bodkin.

5. Fill a piping bag with some white royal icing and a no.0 piping tube and pipe two dots between each of the pink sugarpaste sections.

6. Following the section on double extension work with open panels, colour 225gm (1/2lb) icing with some rose pink food colour and pipe the bridge and extension work.

7. Colour 112gm (1/4lb) icing, green. Fill a greaseproof bag with some of this icing but do not add a piping tube. Press the icing to the end of the bag then flatten this between your thumb and first finger. Cut the end of the bag into a V.

Press out some icing, gradually lifting the bag and removing the pressure. The icing should form a point. If it does not, cut the bag a little more. The shape created should resemble a small leaf.

8. Pipe two leaves onto the open section of bridge leaving a small gap in the centre for the flower.

9. Place some green icing into a second greaseproof bag without a piping tube and cut off the tip to form a small round hole about the size of a no.1 tube.

10. Pipe a small cone of green icing just clear of the first layer of extension work strings and between the piped leaves. Attach a single unwired blossom in each gap.

11. Pipe a dot of pale pink icing into the centre of each flower.

12. Fill a piping bag fitted with a no. 00 piping tube and the same coloured icing as used for the outer layer of dropped strings.

13. To Pipe the open panels begin by piping the back two alternate slanted strings first then bring each pair of slanted strings slightly forward of the last. Neaten the bottom edge with a paintbrush.

14. Trace the pattern for the lace and follow the section on lace to pipe the pieces. Powder the top edge of each using a little candy pink and cornflour.

15. Attach the lace in groups of three over the top edge of the extension work. Leave the open panels clear. Pipe a dot on the central top of each open panel and gently powder with pink.

16. Fill a piping bag with some pale pink icing and a no.0 piping tube. Pipe a line of icing around each scallop of extension work.

17. Place something under one side of the cake thus tipping it forward. Pipe a deep scallop following the curve of each open panel. Turn the cake to ensure each scallop is the same depth and angle from the cake.

18. Assemble the flower spray on top.

19. Attach the pink ribbon around the edge of the cake drum. Attach the gold edged ribbon around the centre of the pink ribbon.

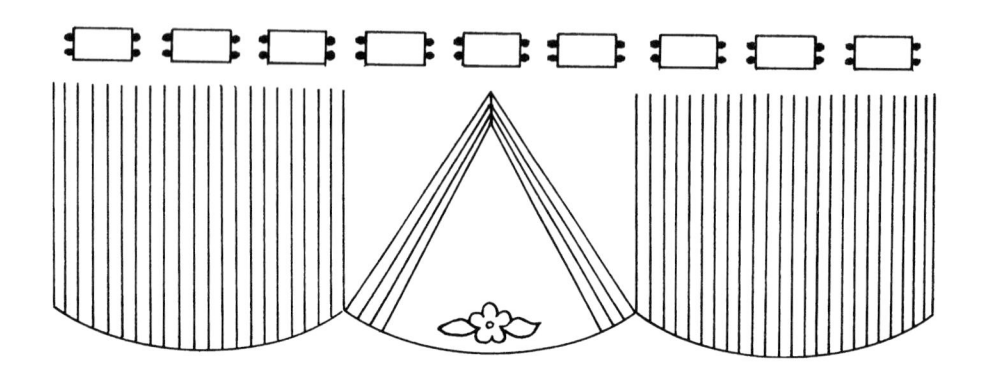

Merry Christmas

The colours on this cake are vibrant and along with its unusual extension work, designed for "shadow play", make it a striking cake for Christmas. This cake is featured on page 54.

Additional equipment

3mm (1/8") white ribbon
3mm (1/8") red ribbon
12mm (1/2") green ribbon
2 piped Fir Cones
Merry Christmas stencil
2 Christmas Roses
6 Holly Leaves
Food colours: Paste - Christmas red, mint green

Find the following sections in the book

Floating extension work in sections	page 46
Lace	page 57
Pattern making floating extension work	page 24

To decorate the cake

1. Follow the section pattern making for floating extention work to make the pattern for the cake side and floating bridge using the example given as a guide. Inscribe the side pattern onto the cake.

2. Fill a piping bag with some white royal icing and a no.1 piping tube and pipe a snail's trail around the base of the cake.

3. Arrange the Christmas Roses, leaves and fir cones on top of the cake.

4. Place the stencil onto the cake and using a crank handled palette knife, cover the cut out Merry Christmas with a layer of Christmas red royal icing.

Draw the knife over the cut out words to level and neaten the icing, then very carefully lift one edge of the stencil and remove.

Take great care that you do not move the stencil whilst working through it.

5. Attach the white ribbon above the snail's trail. Colour 112gm (1/4lb) royal icing Christmas red and pipe evenly spaced dots around the ribbon. Reserve the remaining icing.

6. Trace one floating bridge section and following the instructions for floating extension work on page 46 attach the bridge sections to the cake.

7. Colour 225gm (1/2lb) royal icing green and using a no.00 piping tube, pipe one half of each triangular section. Reserve remaining icing.

8. Use white royal icing and a no.00 piping tube to pipe the other halves of the triangles.

9. Very gently remove the bridge in small sections, pipe very soft dots of royal icing the same colour as the strings to connect them in pairs.

Handy Tip

When you reach the point at which the bridge joins the cake ensure all the dropped strings are free, then ease away the final connecting piece of bridge with a pin. You may need to cover up any marks with a little soft royal icing.

---

10. Follow the section on lace and use the same size piping tube as you used to pipe the dropped strings to pipe the tree and star shapes. One half of each tree should be green the other white. Pipe the stars all white. Pipe small dots of Christmas red on the points of each tree and star.

11. Attach the trees and stars to the top of the extension work. The stars at the highest points and the trees at the lowest. Lean the stars slightly outwards.

12. Fill a piping bag with some white royal icing and a no.1 piping tube and pipe a snail's trail around the outer edge of the cake.

Attach the green ribbon around the cake drum with a little royal icing.

88

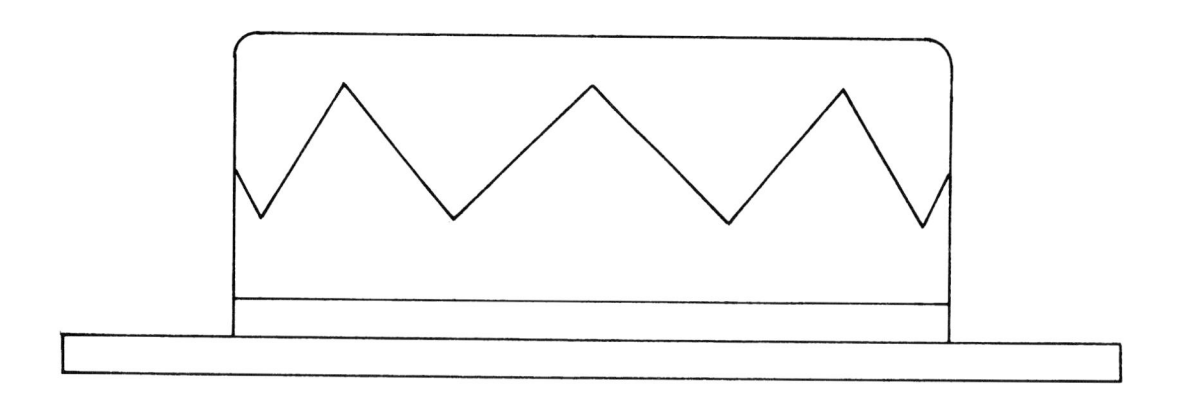

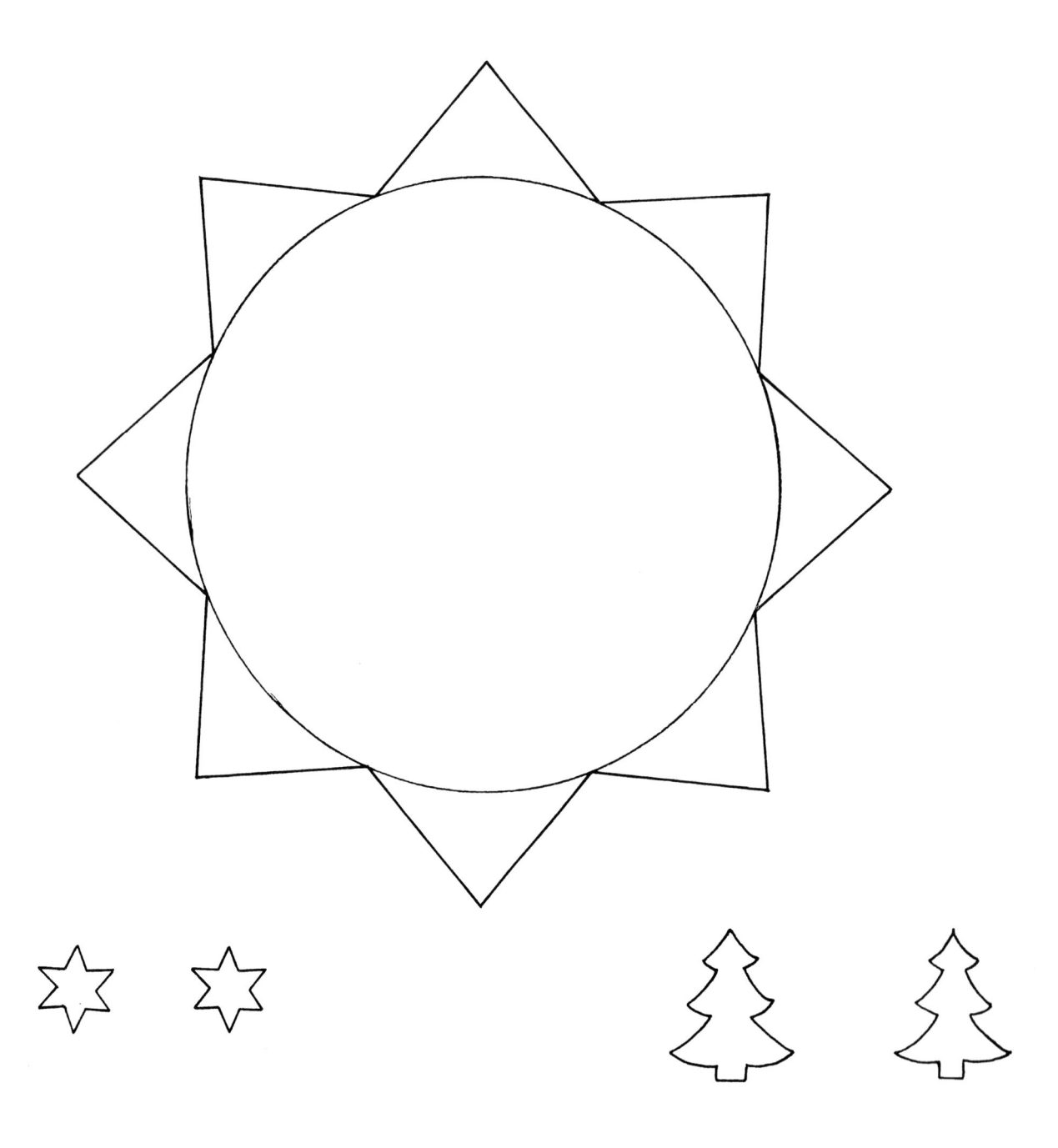

Lullaby

This cake with its pretty extension work and dainty flowers is ideal for a baby girl's christening. This cake is featured on page 51.

Additional equipment
150mm (6") oval cake covered with white sugarpaste on an 225mm (9") cake drum covered with pink sugarpaste
3mm ($^1/_8$") pale pink ribbon
12mm ($^1/_2$") pale pink ribbon
babies head mould
Leaves, orchids, spray roses and anonymous flowers
Food colour: Paste- paprika, blue, dark brown
              Liquid - rose pink

Find the following section in the book
Lace   page 57

To decorate the cake

1. Trace the pattern for the cake side onto a piece of adding machine roll and inscribe this onto the cake.

2. Assemble the flowers on the top of the cake.

3. Make a pillow for the baby's head by moulding a piece of sugarpaste the size of a hazelnut into a circle approximately 12mm ($^1/_2$") in diameter. Dampen the cake and lay the pillow in place.

4. Roll out some pink sugarpaste and cut into thin strips. Frill one edge and cover the pillow in layers.

5. Dust a small piece of sugarpaste with cornflour and press this into the baby's head mould. Remove and paint the skin with a little paprika. Paint the eyes blue, lips deeper paprika and rose pink, hair dark brown. Place the head on the pillow.

6. Take a piece of pink sugarpaste and shape into a cone dampen the cake and place this with the thicker end at the base of the baby's head.

7. Roll out a rectangle of white sugarpaste and frill the edge, dampen the pink cone and lay the blanket on top turning down the top edge. Pipe the initial of the baby's name on top and paint silver.

8. Fill a piping bag with some white royal icing and a no.1 piping tube and pipe a snail's trail around the base of the cake. Attach the 3mm ($^1/_8$") pale pink ribbon above this.

9. Trace the pattern for the medallions and using a no.00 piping tube and some pale pink royal icing pipe the inner section.

Fill a piping bag with white royal icing and a no.0 piping tube and pipe the oval surround, overpipe this. Pipe a line of royal icing along one bracket and leave to dry.

10. Attach each medallion to the cake's side where indicated, using the bracket as a support. (see figure 1) Remove the bracket when dry.

11. Trace the pattern for one curve and place this under cellophane. Fill a piping bag with white royal icing and a no.0 piping tube and pipe one curve. Overpipe this. Leave to dry then remove.

12. Assemble three brackets between two of the medallions. (see figure 2)

13. Place one curve onto the brackets and attach with a dot of icing to the same depth on each medallion. The curve should form a downward loop. If it is too long, remove a little icing from each end of the loop with a little water and then attach it to the medallions.

14. Pipe one layer of slanting dropped strings then another slanting the opposite way on top.

15. Remove the bridge and pipe small dots where two strings meet.

16. Trace the pattern for the lace and follow the section on lace to pipe the lace pieces. Use the same piping tube to pipe the lace, as you used to pipe the dropped strings. Place a dot of pink run-out icing where indicated. Leave to dry 30 minutes.

17. Attach the lace to the medallions and top edge of the floating extension work. Two pieces of lace are angled toward the cake drum with the central piece angled upwards towards the cake's top.

18. Using a no.00 piping tube, pipe embroidery above the lace and on the cake drum.

19. A flower and leaf may be added to the cake drum if desired. Finish by attaching a pale pink ribbon around the cake drum.

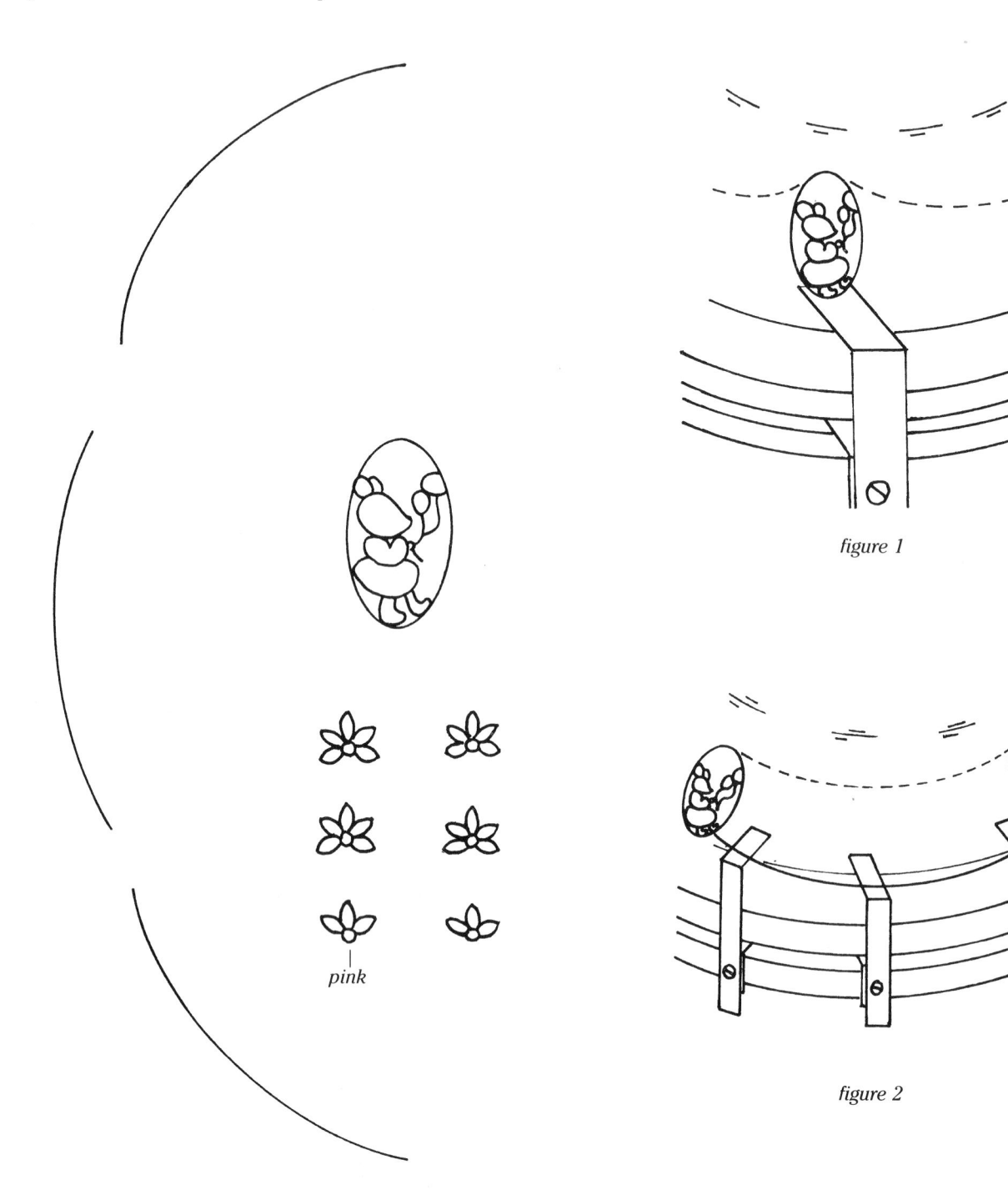

pink

figure 1

figure 2

Castle in the Air

This dainty cake is perfect for any birthday, as the decoration looks striking on any coloured background. It features floating extension work, with a shaped top and a fairytale castle in the clouds.

The extension work and lace were worked using a no.00 tube, with the castle being piped directly onto the cake in built up pressure piping. Always complete the top of your cake first, excluding any lace, as this helps to reduce the risk of damaging your side decoration.

The board may be covered with sugarpaste if wished.

This cake is featured on page 45.

Additional equipment
200mm (8") round cake covered with mulberry coloured sugarpaste on an 275mm (11") cake drum
Cut out flower blossoms 16 small, 16 medium

Find the following sections in the book
Floating extension work on a continuous line   page 48
Pressure piped built up run-outs   page 37
Lace   page 57

To decorate the cake

1. Trace the castle pattern onto a piece of thin card. Cut around the traced pattern and place it onto your cake, making sure it is in the centre.

2. Score around the edge of the pattern. Repeat using the curved pattern again making sure it is centred on the cake top.

3. Follow the section for built up pressure piped run-outs to complete the run-out castle. Using a no.0 tube pipe over the remaining scored lines to create the effect of clouds. Leave the outer curved circle clear.

4. Following the section on lace, pipe the lace pieces. Use the same size piping tube as you intend to use to pipe the dropped strings. Leave to dry.

5. Trace the side pattern onto adding machine roll and taking care to line up the scallops on the sides with those on top of the cake, mark this pattern onto your cake side.

6. Use a no.2 piping tube to pipe a snail's trail border around the base of the cake. Position the cut out blossoms. (see figure 1) Pipe small pink centres into the flowers.

7. Trace the pattern for the floating bridge.

8. Follow the section on floating extension work to pipe your bridge. Pipe this in four sections. Then complete the floating extension work.

Use a slightly stiffer icing to pipe the deeper dropped strings as they will not stretch quite so much.

9. Pipe a dot pattern around the dropped strings and remove the base, then finish with a second row of dots.

10. Pipe random dots between the top of the extension work and the scored curved line on top of the cake.

11. Fix the lace pieces onto this scored line, ensuring the corners are attached first. Repeat on the sides just above the extension work. Make sure the lace is evenly spaced.

12. Pipe fine embroidery lines where the lace meets the cake's surface.

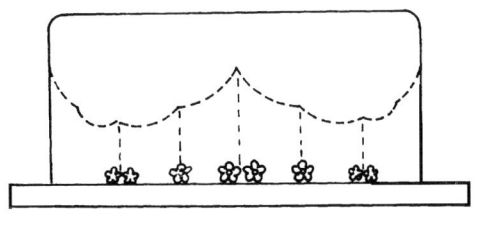

figure 1

92

Cream Sensation

This sophisticated cake is quite enchanting. Brush embroidery, flowers and floating extension work all combine to produce a truly beautiful cake for that once in a lifetime occasion. The colour scheme of pure white on a cream background, was complemented by flowers worked in shades of cream, with variegated ivy leaves. This cake is featured on pages 82 and 83.

Additional equipment
150mm (6") cake on a 225mm (9") cake drum
250mm (10") cake on a 350mm (14") cake drum
Both cakes and boards covered with ivory coloured sugarpaste. Leave to dry 48 hours.
3mm (1/8") ribbon
1 set of plastic dividers
1 round posy of flowers

Find the following sections in the book
Brush embroidery   page 38
Floating extension work on a continuous bridge   page 48
Lace   page 57
Trouble shooting   page 56

To decorate the cake

1. Using a no.1 piping tube, pipe a snail's trail around the base of both cakes and attach a 3mm (1/8") ribbon just above the piping. Leave for 30 minutes.

2. Take a piece of adding machine roll and wrap it round the cake until it just fits. Make sure it is the same depth as the cake. This may mean cutting a strip off one side. Fold in half and draw a straight line 6mm (1/4") below the top of one end of the adding machine roll, to a point two thirds of the depth of the cake. Use the pattern shown as a guide.

3. Place the appropriate pattern around each cake, securing it at the back (the highest point) with a pin.

4. Following the section on brush embroidery, trace the pattern for the brush embroidery and place this in the centre front of the cake. The outer edges of the pattern should rest 12mm (1/2") above the scored floating extension work line.

5. Score the minimum of guide lines onto the cake, then work the brush embroidery using white royal icing.

6. Trace the pattern for the floating bridge lines. Following the section on floating extension work on a continuous bridge, pipe the bridge lines in four sections. Leave to dry.

7. Assemble the brackets around the cake so that the floating bridge rests approximately 6mm (1/4") above the cake board. Arrange the bridge around the cake, taking care that the centre of one wide curve is in the centre front of the cake. Add stops and join the bridge lines.

8. Following the section on piping floating extension work dropped strings, pipe the dropped strings beginning with the centre back.

Handy tip

Use a stiffer icing for the longer strings as this does not stretch quite so easily making deep strings less likely to break when being piped. Gradually soften the icing as you progress to the shorter strings.

9. Using a no.0 or 00 piping tube and soft royal icing, pipe the dot and heart pattern onto the strings. Do not let the piping tube touch the dropped strings, as they break very easily. Refer to the trouble shooting section if you break any dropped strings.

10. Pipe a dot pattern around the dropped strings and remove the bridge. Finish with a second row of dots.

11. Trace the pattern for the lace off-pieces and following the section on lace, pipe them using white royal icing and the same size piping tube as used for the dropped strings. Pipe the lace.

12. Attach one row of lace to the top edge of the extension work. (see figure 1)

13. Attach a second row of lace to the top of the first. Gradually angle this row of lace in a gentle downward curve from a high point in the centre back, to a low point in the centre front. (see figure 2) Pipe a dot on top of each lace piece.

14. Place the set of plastic dividers containing a spray of flowers on top of the bottom tier. Make sure these dividers are in the centre.

15. Place the round posy in the centre of the 150mm (6") cake and assemble on top of the divider.

16. Take care to line up the centre fronts of both cakes and make sure that the top tier is centred over the bottom.

This two tier cake will cut into approximately 88 pieces.

TOP TIER

BOTTOM TIER

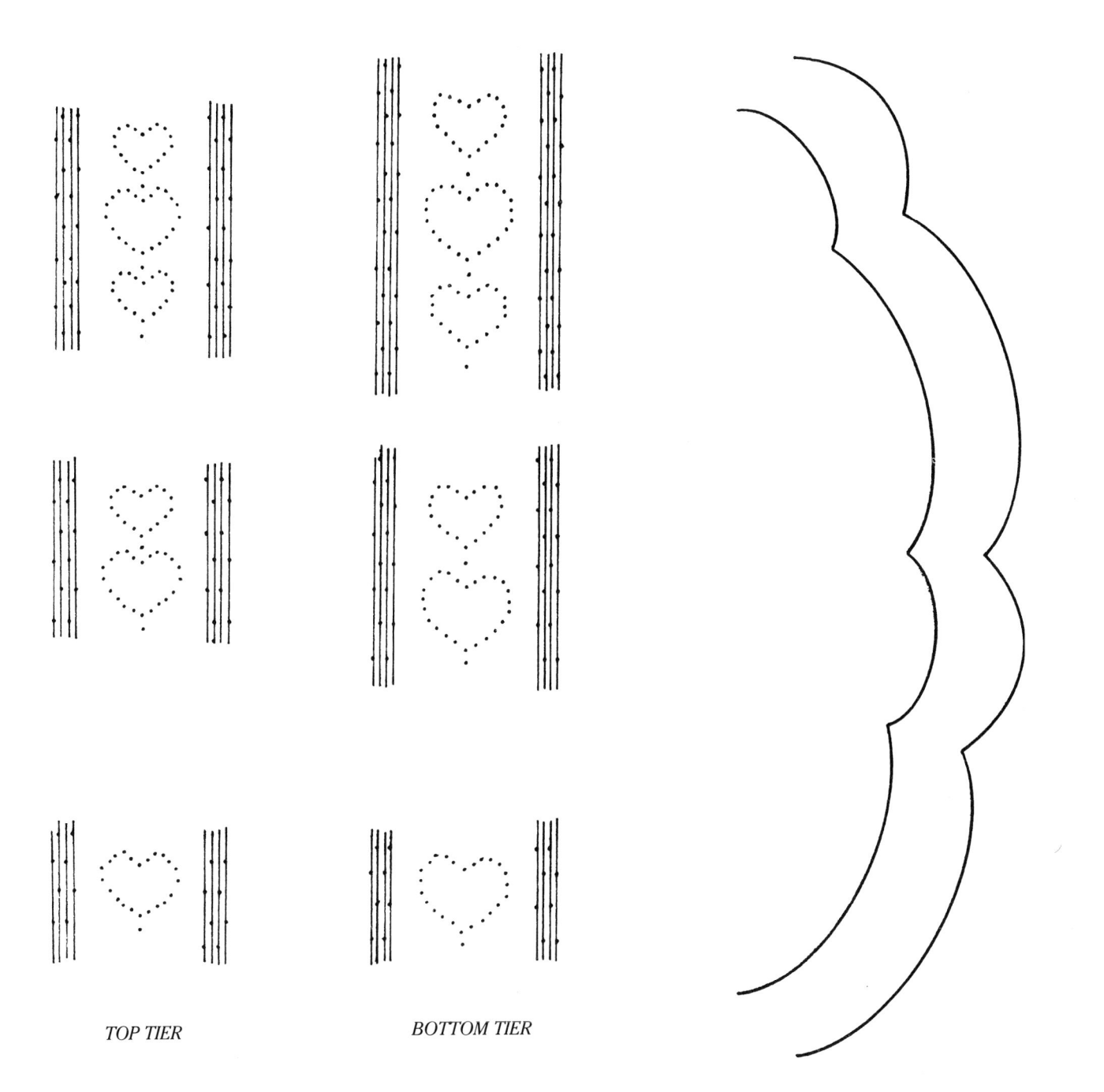

TOP TIER *BOTTOM TIER*

95

TOP TIER

BOTTOM TIER

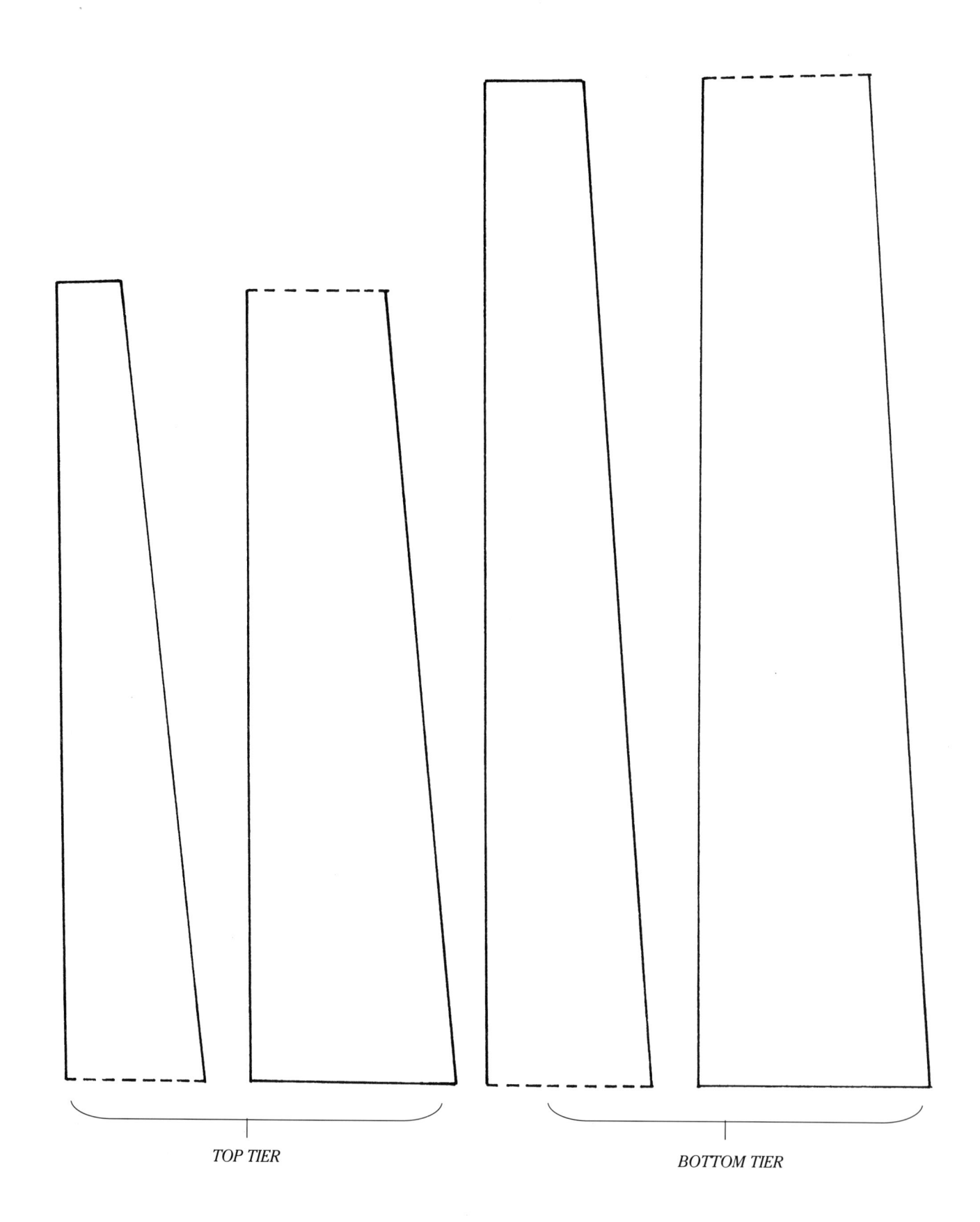

SIDE PATTERN

Best of friends

This pretty birthday cake combines a pressure piped run-out with ribbon insertion, embroidery, lace and tiered floating extension work and is featured on page 35.

Additional equipment

200mm (8") oval cake covered with marzipan
300mm (12") cake drum
3mm (1/8") blue ribbon
12mm (1/2") velvet blue ribbon
Food colours: Powder- peach, sparkle white.
     Paste - chestnut, black paprika, blue,
     mulberry, dark brown, bitter lemon

Find the following sections in the book

Pressure piped run-outs	page 33
Tiered with a double skirt	page 69
Covering with sugarpaste	page 16
Ribbon insertion	page 26
Lace	page 57

To decorate the cake

1. Place the 200mm (8") cake on a moveable, flexible surface and cover with a thin layer of white sugarpaste. Leave to dry for 48 hours.

2. Cover the cake drum with a thin layer of white sugarpaste.

3. Mix some peach and sparkle white powder together. Make sure there are no separate grains of colour. Use a soft piece of foam to powder the top of the cake.

4. Following the section on pressure piped run-outs, pipe the cat and toddler onto the cake. Leave to dry for 48 hours.

5. Cut a piece of greaseproof paper to fit over the cat and toddler and place in position. Following the section covering with sugarpaste, roll out some white sugarpaste and cover the cake.

6. Use a plaque cutter to cut out the oval shape feeling through the sugarpaste to help with centring.

7. Remove the cut out section and then remove the greaseproof paper. Using your fingers, gently stroke each scallop down towards the cake. This will produce a round shape the end of which just touches the cake's surface.

8. Gently peel the cake from the flexible surface and centre it onto the sugarpaste covered cake drum. Using a no.2 piping tube, pipe a row of small shells around the base. Attach a ribbon just above these shells.

9. Following the section on ribbon insertion, insert small pieces of blue ribbon at equal distances from the edge of each scallop.

10. Using the chart, paint the run-out.

11. Fill a piping bag with white royal icing and a no.0 piping tube. Pipe a fine line around the edge of each scallop. Pipe three small dots on either end of each piece of ribbon to anchor it in place.

12. Following the section on tiered with a double skirt, make the pattern for the cake's side and mark this onto the cake.

13. Pipe a snail's trail around the bottom edge of the cake and attach a 3mm (1/8") ribbon above it. Pipe the extension work following the section on tiered with a double skirt but omitting the under skirt.

14. Pipe the dot pattern onto the dropped strings and remove the bridge. Finish with another rows of dots.

15. Trace the pattern for the lace and following the section on lace pipe these pieces. Remove and attach to the top edge of the extension work.

16. Using a no.00 piping tube pipe the embroidery following the pattern given.

17. Using a no.1 piping tube pipe a line of shells around the outer edge of the cake drum. Attach a blue velvet ribbon to the side of the cake drum.

Colour chart

Toddler

skin-very pale paprika

eyes-dark brown

hair-chestnut and bitter lemon

nose and mouth-paprika

ribbon-pale blue

sole-paprika

shoe-black

upper boot-paprika

dress-highlight shadows with very pale blue

Cat

chest and ear-pale mulberry

mouth-very dark brown

body and face-dark brown

paws-highlight toes dark brown

Kentish Scene

This cake is most unusual with its Oast Houses and Kentish rural scenes. The extension work with its theme of sky, is masculine enough to please the male of the family. This cake is featured on page 72.

Additional equipment
200mm (8") round cake on an 275mm (11") cake drum both covered with white sugarpaste
2 blocks of wood 1 - 15mm ($^5/_8$") deep and 1 - 9mm ($^3/_8$") deep
Food colours to paint pictures: Powders - apple green, cornflower blue

Find the following sections in the book
Outlined run-outs   page 31
Floating extension work on an inverted bridge   page 73
Pattern making for floating extension work   page 24

To decorate the cake

1. Trace the oast house run-out pattern shown and follow the section on outlined run-outs to complete this run-out. Leave to dry 12 hours.

2. Paint the run-out and leave to dry 24 hours.

3. Mix a small quantity of blue power food colour with some cornflour to create a pale blue shade. Take a piece of soft foam and dip this into the powder. Tap the foam to remove any excess powder, then dust half of the cake's top with this.

Handy Tip

Use an old paintbrush to mix powders. Ensure no stray grains of the pure colour are left before use. When applying powder to the cake use small circular movements.

---

4. Following step 3 powder the bottom half of the cake's top with pale green.

5. Place two blocks of wood one 15mm deep, the other 9mm deep on top of the cake. Space them approximately 50mm (2") apart. Gently lay the run-out on top ensuring the deeper wood block is under the roof. (see figure 1)

6. Using some white royal icing and a no.00 tube, pipe dropped strings from the edge of the run-out to the cake. Neaten the ends with a paintbrush.

7. Using a no.0 tube, pipe a snail's trail around the top edge of the run-out and the bottom edge of the dropped strings.

8. Follow the section pattern making to make the side pattern. Mark the points of the top edge at least half the depth of the cake side.

9. Follow the section on pattern making for floating extension work and use the example given to make your bridge pattern. Pipe your bridge.

10. Paint each scene to form a miniature picture within one scallop.

11. Complete the floating extension work in blue royal icing following the instruction in the section on an inverted bridge.

12. Remove the bridge and finish with dots joining the dropped strings in pairs.

13. Using a no.00 piping tube, following the section on lace to pipe poor man's lace around the top edge of the extension work.

14. Using a no.0 piping tube, pipe a snail's trail over the edge of the poor man's lace to finish.

ROOF   RUN-OUT   BASE
WOOD   WOOD

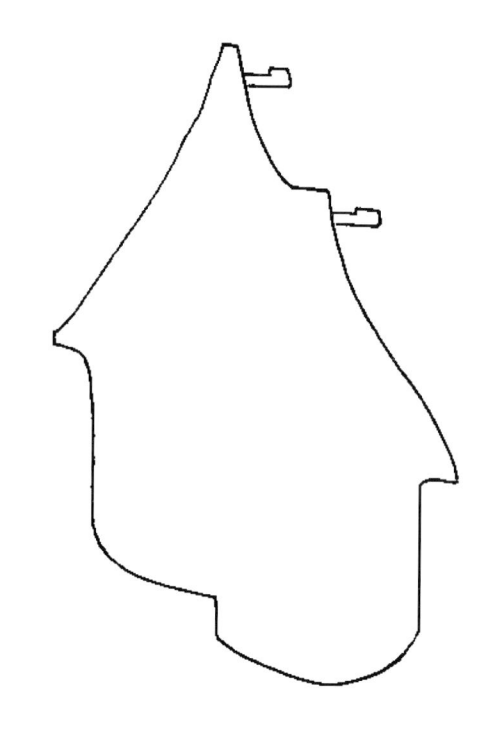

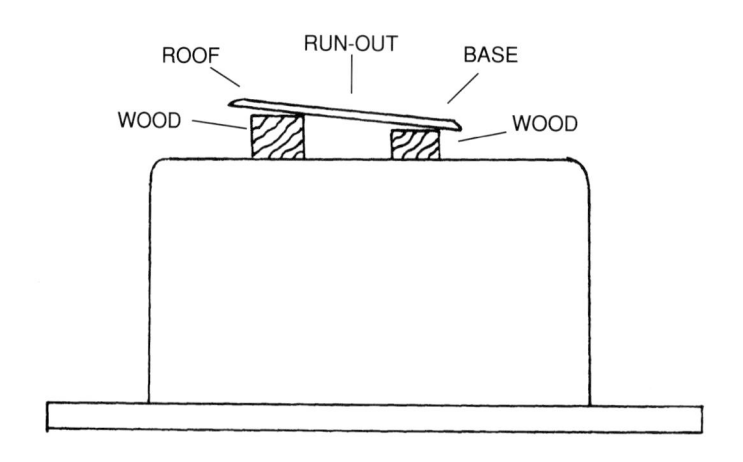

Golden Showers

This elegant cake has delecate floating extension work edged with lace. The embroidery is combined with lemon ribbon insertion and each tier is enhanced with beautiful golden sugar lilies. The cake was made for an English Professor and his wife. It is featured on the cover of the book and on pages 52 and 53.

Additional equipment
150mm (6") cake on an 200mm (8") cake drum
200mm (8") cake on an 250mm (10") cake drum
250mm (10") cake on an 350mm (14") cake drum
3mm (1/8") yellow ribbon
12mm (1/2") yellow ribbon
Three sprays of flowers
Food colours: liquid lemon

Find the following sections in the book
Ribbon insertion   page 26
Pattern making   page 24
Floating extention work on a continuous bridge   page 48
Double with inserts   page 70
Double extension work   page 68
Lace   page 57

To decorate the cakes

The instructions given are the same for each cake. Work on one cake at a time.

1. Cover the cake with white sugarpaste.

2. Use one side of a pair of curved crimpers to cut a pattern around the edge of the cake drum.

3. Follow the section pattern making floating extension work to make the pattern for the cake's side. Mark this onto the cake.

4. Follow the section on ribbon insertion and complete the ribbon insertion. Leave to dry for 48 hours.

Handy Tip
Work very gently on fresh sugarpaste as it marks easily.

---

5. Attach 3mm (1/8") wide ribbon around the base of the cake.

Follow the pattern making section double extension work, to make the floating bridge pattern. Make this pattern a circle. Keep the pattern.

6. Follow the section on floating extension work on a continuous bridge, to pipe the first layer of extension work in deep lemon. Finish with dots in the same colour. Reserve the remaining icing.

7. Use a no.00 piping tube and soft pale lemon royal icing to pipe the embroidery onto the dropped strings.

8. Follow the section on double with inserts, to make a second bridge and to pipe the second layer of extension work and make the heart shaped inserts. Use the patterns given as a guide and pale lemon royal icing. Pipe dots onto the strings in a regular pattern. Use pale lemon icing for all of this work.

9. Follow the section on lace to pipe the lace off pieces in white. Pipe the dots in the deep lemon icing used in step 4.

Attach the lace to the top edge of the extension work.

10. Using a no.00 piping tube and white royal icing, pipe the embroidery and dots around the ribbon insertion.

11. Using a no.1 piping tube and the deep lemon icing from step 4, pipe small curves around the outer edge of the sugarpaste cake drum.

12. Finish with an arrangement of flowers on each tier and attach a yellow ribbon to the side of the cake drum.

To make the top decoration

This decoration is designed to be removed from the cake after the wedding, to be kept by the Bride and Groom as a memento of their day. It is therefore mounted on a 100mm (4") round sugarpaste covered cake board and attached to the cake with a dab of royal icing. The edge is covered with lemon ribbon and overpiped with shells using a no.2 piping tube.

1. Take a 100mm (4") round cake card 4mm thick and cover this with a thin layer of sugarpaste.

2. Trace the pattern for one panel of the top decoration and place this under a sheet of very flat cellophane.

3. Fill one piping bag with white royal icing and a no.0 piping tube and another bag with white royal icing and a no.00 piping tube.

4. Use the no.00 piping tube to pipe the central heart and scroll design. Use the no.0 piping tube to pipe the centre line and base. Make sure all the lines touch each other at some points.

5. Use the no.0 piping tube, to pipe the curved line touching the outer edges of the hearts and scrolls.

6. Use the no.00 piping tube to pipe the tiny scrolls. Make sure they all touch the thicker no.0 line. Use the no.0 piping tube to pipe the outer line. Leave to dry for 2 hours. Remove from the cellophane and turn over. Overpipe the design using the same step by step sequence and piping tubes as before.

Make four panels and at least two spares.

Handy Tip

Lay the panel onto a thin piece of velvet to prevent it moving while you overpipe it.

To assemble the decoration

1. Trace around the base of the covered cake board and cut out. Carefully fold the cut out circle into four.

2. Place this circle on top of the cake board and mark along the four creased lines to give a guide for the placement of the four pieces.

3. Pipe soft dots of icing just short of the centre along one of the marked lines. Gently lift one panel using the brush ends of two paintbrushes to do this. Very gently position the centre of one panel onto the softened iced dots. Pipe a second dot under the back edge of this panel.

4. Support the panel on either side and ensure it is straight. Leave to dry for one hour.

5. Repeat step 3; placing the second panel opposite the first and attached both panels at the centre top, middle and bottom.

6. Remove the supports from the first panel, then repeat step 3 placing the last two panels at 90deg to the first and second panel.

7. Add small sprays of flowers into the spaces formed by the panels.

TAKE VERY GREAT CARE THAT YOU DO NOT TOUCH THE PANELS AT ANY POINT

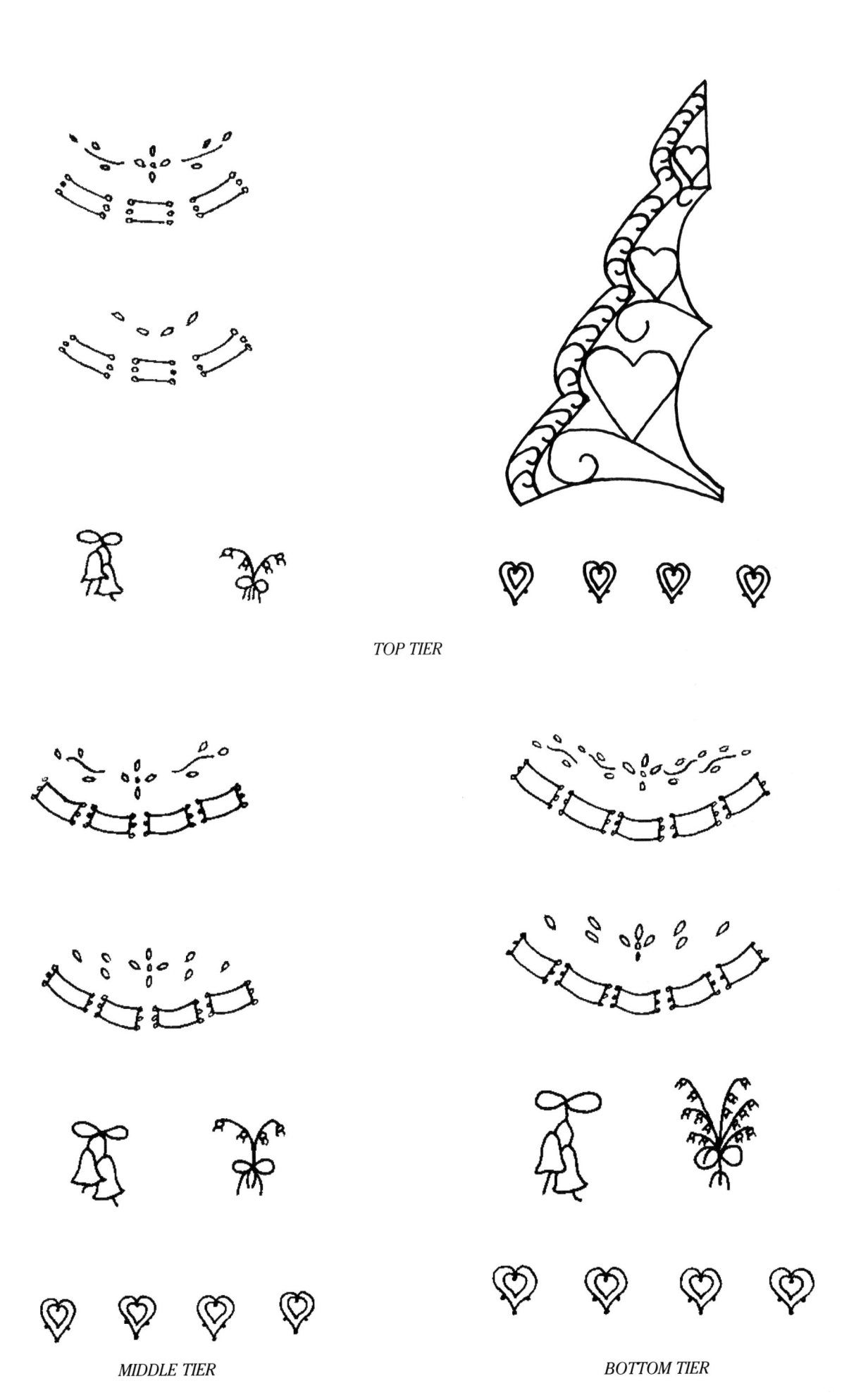

TOP TIER

MIDDLE TIER

BOTTOM TIER

103

True Love

This cake is an enchanting mixture of delicate double tiered extension work, brush embroidery, pressure piping and cut out flowers. It should only be attempted by the very experienced sugarcraft artist as it is a very complex piece of work involving three separate layers of floating extension work and a suspended floating collar on top. It is featured on page 37 and 84.

Additional equipment
200mm (8") round cake covered with marzipan. The cake sides should be at least 75mm (3") deep, 12 mm ($^1/_2$") cake drum
16 cut out flowers
12mm ($^1/_2$") old gold ribbon
Food colours: Powder - peach
                Paste - dark brown, gooseberry, black.
                Liquid - lemon, kingfisher blue, primrose.

Find the following sections in the book
Covering with sugarpaste	page 16
Pressure piped run-outs	page 33
Brush embroidery	page 38
Lace	page 57
Removing the floating bridge to graduate the dropped strings	page 55

To decorate the cake

1. Place the cake onto a moveable, flexible surface. Following the section on covering with sugarpaste, cover the cake with white sugarpaste. Leave to dry for 48 hours.

2. Colour some sugarpaste peach and use this to roll out and thinly cover the cake drum. Leave to dry for 48 hours.

3. Place the cake onto the covered cake drum, taking care to centre it.

4. To complete the run-out, trace the pattern for the branch and flowers and inscibe these onto the cake.

5. Mix the peach powder with an equal amount of cornflour and use this to powder the centre of the cake.

6. Trace the pattern for the inner edge of the suspended floating collar and inscribe this onto the cake.

7. Trace the pattern for the birds and a separate pattern for the wings. Place these patterns under cellophane. Following the section on pressure piped run-outs, pipe the bird's wings. Leave to dry for 4 hours.

8. Remove from cellophane and following the section on pressure piped run-outs, pipe each bird's body separately inserting the wing while the icing is still soft. Support with small pieces of folded paper until dry. Leave for 48 hours.

9. Paint each bird and remove from cellophane. While the birds are drying, follow the section on brush embroidery to complete the flowers and leaves. Pressure pipe the branch and paint when dry.

10. Pipe three or four dots of royal icing and gently lay bird no. 1 on top. Repeat with bird no. 2 taking care to overlay the first bird slightly. Pipe in the feet, using a no.2 piping tube, then paint.

11. Pipe two leaves in each alternate scallop on top of the cake, adding a blossom in the centre of these.

12. Trace the outer pattern of the suspended floating collar and place this under very flat cellophane. Pipe each curve separately using a no.0 piping tube.

13. Assemble the brackets around the cake top (figure 1) and lay the curves on top. Using a no.0 piping tube and softened royal icing join each scallop to the next. Lifting the centre of the scallop opposite each flower and inserting enough pieces of thin card between it and the bracket, to raise the scallop higher than the top of the flower.

14. Use a no.00 piping tube and slightly stiffer royal icing, to pipe raised strings from the inscribed line on the cake top to the floating bridge. When complete leave to dry for 12 hours. Pipe the first layer of dots and remove the bridge in very small sections. Pipe in the second layer of dots every 12mm(½").

15. Follow the section on lace to pipe the lace off-pieces. Powder the dots with peach then remove from the cellophane. Use two paintbrushes to lift and attach the lace just above the top of the raised strings.

To work the sides

1. Follow the section pattern making tiered to make the pattern for the cake's side and inscribe this onto the cake.

2. Using a no.1 piping tube and white royal icing, pipe a snail's trail around the bottom edge of the cake. Pipe two leaves and insert a flower under every alternate scallop opposite those on top.

3. Follow the section on double floating extension work to make your pattern for the floating bridges. The first bridge should be a complete circle, the second should contain 16 scallops.

4. Pipe the first layer of floating extension work. Follow the section to graduate the dropped strings to raise the strings in gentle curves over the flower. Pipe the second bridge in four sections.

5. Replace the brackets and lay the second bridge on top. Take care to line up the points of the curves with the points of the first layer.

6. Colour 112gms(¼ lb) royal icing peach and using a no.00 piping tube, pipe three dropped strings the centre one being piped from the point of each scallop to the point of each bridge scallop.

7. Fill in the scallops without a flower with straight dropped strings.

8. Follow the pattern to fill in the alternate scallops. Remove the bridge and join the dropped strings in pairs.

> ### *Handy Tip*
> When piping the dots, work from each open section towards the point of the scallop. This will help to hide any dropped strings which may be single. Pipe a dot on the end of these.

9. Using a no.00 piping tube and some very soft peach royal icing, pipe an even number of tiny dots onto the slanting dropped strings as shown in the pattern.

10. Replace the brackets following the section on tiered floating extension work, pipe a second tier of floating extension work. Make sure you pipe one dropped string in peach royal icing from the point on the inscribed scallop to the point of each floating bridge scallop above the lower coloured dropped strings.

11. Overpipe the alternate scallops following the pattern.

12. Using a no.00 piping tube and some very soft peach royal icing, pipe an even number of coloured dots down the centre dropped string as shown in the pattern.

13. Following the section on lace, pipe the lace off-pieces and powder the dots with peach. Attach to the top edge of the floating extension work.

14. Using a no.00 piping tube, follow the pattern to pipe the embroidery.

15. Attach a ribbon around the cake's side.

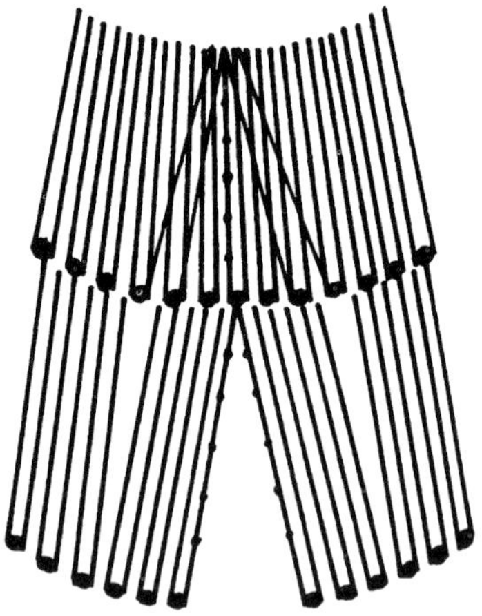

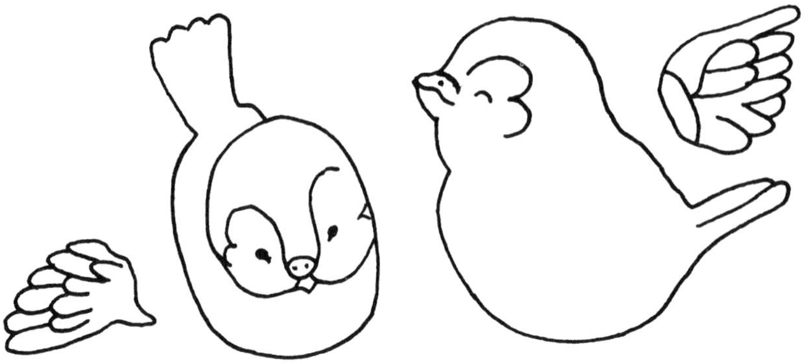

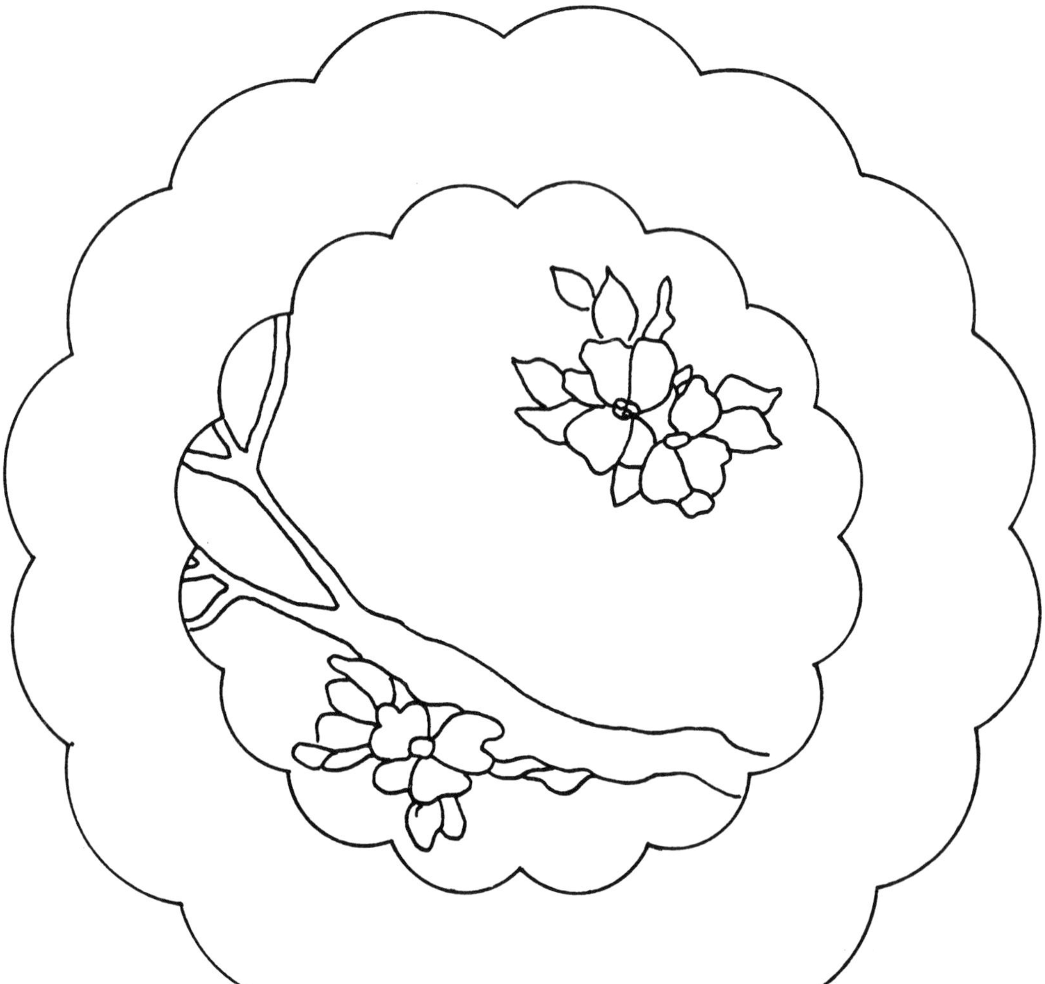

Tables of Quantities

Sponge Cake

Ingredients

IMPERIAL							METRIC					
shape	size	caster sugar	marg.	sr flour	eggs	warm water	size	caster sugar	marg.	sr flour	eggs	warm water
Oval	6"	5	5	5	2½	½tsp	150mm	140gms	140gms	140gms	2½	½ tsp
Round Oct.	6"	6	6	6	3	½tsp	150mm	168gms	168gms	168gms	3	½tsp
Sq.,Hex., Heart	6"	8	8	8	4	1tsp	150mm	225gms	225gms	225gms	4	1tsp
Oval	8"	8	8	8	4	1tsp	200mm	225gms	225gms	225gms	4	1tsp
Round, Oct.	8"	12	12	12	6	1tsp	200mm	336gms	336gms	336gms	6	1tsp
Sq., Hex., Heart	8"	16	16	16	8	2tsp	200mm	450gms	450gms	450gms	8	2tsp
Oval	10"	12	12	12	6	1tsp	250gms	336gms	336gms	336gms	6	1tsp
Round, Oct.	10"	22	22	22	11	2tsp	250mm	616gms	616gms	616gms	11	2tsp
Sq., Hex., Heart	10"	24	24	24	12	3tsp	250mm	675gms	675gms	675gms	12	3tsp
Oval	12"	16	16	16	8	2tsp	300mm	450gms	450gms	450gms	8	2tsp
Round, Oct.	12"	26	26	26	13	3tsp	300mm	730gms	730gms	730gms	13	3tsp
Sq., Hex., Heart	12"	28	28	28	14	3tsp	300mm	787gms	787gms	787gms	14	3tsp

Rich Fruit Cake

Ingredients

shape	size	caster sugar	butter	srflour	ground almonds	chopped blanched almonds	currents	sultanas	raisins	mixed peel	glace cherries quartered	milk	eggs	nutmeg	mixed spice	treacle	brandy	grated lemon rind
oval	150mm	70gms	70gms	91gms	7gms	7gms	70gms	70gms	56gms	21gms	21gms	6mls	1½	large pinch	large pinch	6mls	10mls	large pinch
	6"	2½oz	2½oz	3¼oz	¼oz	¼oz	2½oz	2½oz	2oz	¾oz	¾oz	1tsp	1½	large pinch	large pinch	1¼tsp	2tsp	large pinch
round, oct.	150mm	112gms	112gms	140gms	14gms	14gms	112gms	112gms	84gms	28gms	28gms	13mls	2	large pinch	1ml	10mls	12½mls	large pinch
	6"	4oz	4oz	5oz	½oz	½oz	4oz	4oz	3oz	1oz	1oz	2½tsp	2	large pinch	¼tsp	2tsp	2½tsp	large pinch
sq.,hex., heart	150mm	140gms	140gms	182gms	21gms	21gms	140gms	140gms	112gms	35gms	35gms	13mls	2½	large pinch	1ml	13mls	15mls	large pinch
	6"	5oz	5oz	6½oz	¾oz	¾oz	5oz	5oz	4oz	1¼oz	1¼oz	2½tsp	2½	large pinch	¼tsp	2½tsp	3tsp	large pinch
oval	200mm	112gms	112gms	140gms	14gms	14gms	112gms	112gms	84gms	28gms	28gms	13mls	2	large pinch	1ml	10mls	12½mls	large pinch
	8"	4oz	4oz	5oz	½oz	½oz	4oz	4oz	3oz	1oz	1oz	2½tsp	2	large pinch	¼tsp	2tsp	2½tsp	large pinch
round, oct.	200mm	225gms	225gms	280gms	28gms	28gms	225gms	225gms	168gms	56gms	56gms	20mls	4	1ml	2½mls	20mls	25mls	¼lemon
	8"	8oz	8oz	10oz	1oz	1oz	8oz	8oz	6oz	2oz	2oz	1tbsp	4	¼tsp	½tsp	1tbsp	5tsp	¼lemon
sq., hex., heart	200mm	308gms	308gms	392gms	42gms	42gms	308gms	308gms	239gms	84gms	84gms	28mls	5½	1ml	3½mls	28mls	30mls	¼lemon
	8"	11oz	11oz	14oz	1½oz	1½oz	11oz	11oz	8½oz	3oz	3oz	1½tbsp	5½	¼tsp	¾tsp	1½tbsp	6tsp	¼ lemon
oval	250mm	225gms	225gms	280gms	28gms	28gms	225gms	225gms	168gms	56gms	56gms	20mls	4	1ml	2½mls	20mls	25mls	¼ lemon
	10"	8oz	8oz	10oz	1oz	1oz	8oz	8oz	6oz	2oz	2oz	1tbsp	4	¼tsp	½tsp	1tbsp	5tsp	¼ lemon
round, oct.	250mm	392gms	392gms	492gms	49gms	49gms	392gms	392gms	308gms	98gms	98gms	35mls	7	2½mls	5mls	35mls	35mls	½ lemon
	10"	14oz	14oz	17½oz	1¾oz	1¾oz	14oz	14oz	11oz	3½oz	3½oz	1¾mls	7	½tsp	1tsp	1¾tbsp	1¾tbsp	½ lemon
sq., hex., heart	250mm	534gms	534gms	675gms	70gms	70gms	534gms	534gms	406gms	133gms	133gms	45mls	10	2½mls	6mls	45mls	60mls	½lemon
	10"	19oz	19oz	24oz	2½oz	2½oz	19oz	19oz	14½oz	4¾gms	4¾gms	2¼tbsp	10	½tsp	1¼tsp	2¼tbsp	3tbsp	½lemon

INDEX

Brush Embroidery	38-39
Cake designs	74
Best of Friends	35, 97-98
Castle in the Air	45, 91-92
Christmas Time	18, 75-76
Congratulations	79-81
Cream Sensation	82-83, 93-96
Golden Showers	52-53, 101-103
Happy Birthday	71, 77-78
Heart's Delight	17, 85-86
Kentish Scene	72, 99-100
Lullaby	51, 89-90
Merry Christmas	54, 87-88
True Love	36, 84, 104-106
Colouring royal icing	12
Consistency	27
Cornelli	30
Covering with marzipan	13-15
Covering with sugarpaste	16, 19-20
Dots	30
Egg white	11
Embroidery	57-59
Enhancing corners	62
Equipment	6-7, 74
Example of piping techniques	30
Exercises, piping	30
Extension work (see fixed, floating)	
Fruit Cake recipe	8-9
Fixed extension work	
bridge	41-42
double	63-64
enhancing corners	62
pattern making	21-23
piping dropped strings	43-44
ribbon inserts	60
shaped bridge	61
slanting strings	65
tiered	66
upside down bridge	67
Floating extension work	
bridge	48
double bridge	68
double with inserts	70
finishing	44, 49-50
graduated dropped strings	55
inverted bridge	73
pattern making	24-25
piping in sections	46-47
tiered	69
Icing (see royal icing)	
Lace	
attaching	59
off pieces	59
piping	57-59
Poor Man's	58
powdering	59
"L" brackets	7
Lining cake tins	8
Lines	30
Outlined run-outs	31-32
Pastillage recipe	77
Pattern making extension work	
double bridge	68
fixed	21-23
floating	24-25
inverted bridge	73
sections	46
Piping	
bags	28-29
cornelli	30
dots	30
dropped strings	43
lace	57-59
lines	30
Poor man's lace	58
snail's trail	30
Powdering	
cake top	98
lace	59, 86, 105
Preparation of cake for covering	10
Pressure piping	33-34
Pressure piping built up	37
Pure albumen powder	12
Removing floating bridge	49-50
Ribbon insertion	26
Royal icing	
colouring	12
consistency	27
making	11, 12
sieving	40
Run-out techniques	
built up	37
outlined	31-32
pressure piped	33-34
Shaping bridge	61
Slanting strings	65
Snail's trail	30
Sponge cake recipe	10
Substitute albumen powder	12
Storage of cakes	10
Table of quantities	
marzipan and sugarpaste	16
fruit cake	108
sponge cake	108
Trouble shooting	56